on Wings & Whimsy

Advance Praise for *On Wings & Whimsy*

"*On Wings & Whimsy* is an invitation to reconnect with your inner child, to take time and press pause in our hectic lives for a moment of reflection. Laugh along with Erika's stories and open your hearts and minds to a fun exploration of self that encourages you to put on rose colored glasses and find the magic and wonder in our (extra)ordinary lives!"

—Jill Gordon, Program Director,
Youth Philanthropy Initiative of Indiana

"*On Wings & Whimsy* is a fun, humorous book that invokes some serious thinking. It's an easy read full of delightful anecdotes, called "Sparks" but it packs a punch with thought-provoking questions. These questions and accompanying journal activities, called "Opportunities," encourage self-reflection providing a great reminder for all of us who are trying to be extraordinary to step back and remember that first we must be extra-ordinary. One of the best ways to learn is through stories, humor, and reflection and this book has it all!"

—Heidi Ham, Vice President,
National AfterSchool Association

on Wings & Whimsy

Finding the **extraordinary** within the ordinary

A product of **The Leadership Program**

by Erika Petrelli

Cover Artwork by Phil Caminiti

Cover and Interior Design by Phil Caminiti

ISBN: 1941916104

ISBN 13: 9781941916100

Contents

Introduction

Thank you for opening this book! I am Erika and we are The Leadership Program, and we welcome you to the pages contained within.

On Wings & Whimsy: Finding the Extraordinary Within the Ordinary is an interactive exploration based on my belief that the most extraordinary moments in life often come disguised as the most ordinary. It is grounded in inspiration (wings) and joy (whimsy).

This book is not necessarily about finding your greatness or unlocking your potential. There are a number of wonderful books that can help you with that, written by people far smarter than I. Instead, it will invite you to step away from what you think you're *supposed* to do or be and just re-discover you—the perfectly imperfect you that already exists.

As a child, I knew this secret. I believed I could fly, and so I put on my wings and disappeared into magical lands. I imagined myself an artist and painted. I cried over hurt feelings or skinned knees and then quickly went back to play. I was armed with those wings of magic and thoughts of whimsy, believing that the world was my playground. I see this in my kids, too. Did you have that experience? Do you see it in any children around you?

As adults, many of us have lost our wings of magic and our thoughts of whimsy. So this book is designed to give you the space to rediscover them. Through reflection and activity, you will be given the opportunity to delight in the wonder that is YOU. At The Leadership Program, one of our core values is to cultivate passion, creativity, joy, and a sense of adventure. And so I invite you to open up your sense of adventure and dive right in.

Here is what you'll find inside:

Sparks: These are jumping-off points, personal stories of
mine designed to make you think, make you laugh, or make you question. You will hear a lot about my two most sparkly pairs of wings & whimsy—my son, Dylan, and my daughter, Marlowe. My husband also makes some appearances, as do family, friends, and coworkers. These stories are mine; they are not meant to be declarations of universal truths. Take what you like and ponder the rest, but carry them gently, my dear sweet ones.

Opportunities: These are challenges, assignments,
and reflections—opportunities for you to reflect on whatever the Spark story triggered in you. Just as my stories share a vulnerable part of me, these Opportunities invite you to be vulnerable and self-reflective too. As one of my coworkers said, "As I grew to know this book, I grew to know myself." Take your time, and allow

yourself to sit with the questions contained within.

A Journal: That's right. Flip to the back of the book and

you will find 100 blank pages all for you. Since the **Opportunities** invite you into personal reflection, we offer you the space for that reflection within the book itself. Use the journal for anything and everything that comes up for you while you're in the midst of this journey of wings and of whimsy.

I hope you find this book to be meaningful, thought provoking, and most importantly, fun. Scribble all over it, cross out things you don't like, and highlight things you love. This is your journey. Do it your way. The only bit of advice I'll offer you is this: The chapters are designed to build upon each other, so following it in sequential order may offer you the most meaningful experience. But if you *are* skipping around, perhaps just make a quick pit stop at the "Overview" section of each chapter so you can ground yourself in its focus. That's it!

Prelude

Each year as spring gives way to summer and academics give way to pools and bike rides, students across the country hear commencement speeches—whether they're graduating from high school or college—at the precipice of "life" beginning. Because that's what commencement means, right? To begin.

Once I started to think about the commencement speech I'd like my son and daughter to hear and the advice that I would give them when they reached this precipice. And as I thought about that, a few things occurred to me: (1) Man, all my advice is very cliché; and (2) Maybe it's not cliché; maybe it's just really good advice that we apparently need to hear over and over and over again; and (3) Why do we wait until pivotal moments like graduation to give these speeches? This "commencing," this is stuff we need to hear when we're commencing turning six and when we're commencing going to camp and when we're commencing another Tuesday and when we're commencing a new job and basically always, because there is always something to commence.

So here's a part of my commencement speech, because it's not just for my children; it's for myself and for you too:

My wish for you is that you understand, deep in your heart, that the most important thing is not to be the smartest or best looking or the one with the most medals or the most money. It's not important to always win. Life is sometimes easy and sometimes hard and sometimes boring and sometimes extraordinary. Live in all of it.

Fill your days with laughter. Love fiercely, and learn that a broken heart does eventually heal. The world is big—explore it. See the sunrise from thirty-five thousand feet, and get your hands dirty from digging in the rich soil of the earth. Understand that happiness will forever elude you if you search for it in other people or places, but it will be your constant companion if you allow space for it to dwell inside of you. Taste rain and also tears. Taste wasabi, which will bring you to tears. Be passionate about something, and always keep that passion nearby, even if it's just a book on your bed stand. Dance often. Don't worry about perfect attendance; in your life there will be many good reasons to play hooky. Understand that most of what makes life extraordinary is hidden inside the most ordinary moments of every day. Don't miss them. Be bold, even if that means risking failure. Trust that failure leads to growth and that, often times, the things we don't get make way for the things we realize we wanted even more. Read as much as you can. Find a strong voice within you, and have the courage to speak up for what is right. Understand that there are many dark parts to this world and that darkness may cast a shadow over you someday—but there is always light too. Keep your eyes focused on finding that light. Even when it's impossible to believe, I promise you that it's there somewhere. Be humble while also knowing that you are truly a gift to this world and all who are lucky enough to know you. Be wary of people who try to tell you otherwise. Talk to cabbies and store clerks and strangers sitting next to you on the plane. Everyone you meet has something to teach you. Be kind. Take pictures. Be in pictures—happily. Don't hide yourself; let the world see you. Say yes to opportunities and adventures. You will regret saying no far more than you will regret saying yes. Don't worry about the size of your wallet or your body; just worry about the size of your heart. Let yourself be surprised. Let yourself be wrong.

And most of all, my biggest wish for you is that you wake up each morning with a content heart because you've surrounded yourself with people whom you love, doing the things that you love, in a place that you love. May you keep joy as the North Star of your compass as you navigate this easy, hard, boring, and extraordinary life. Because even if you are blessed enough to have a very long life, life goes by in a blink. Fill it up.

Congratulations on this commencement, and may whatever is about to begin be simply breathtaking. Now let's begin.

Chapter One: Awaken

Overview

If we are going to discover (or rediscover) the extraordinary in ourselves and around us, we need to make sure we're awake, right?

Most of us have areas in our life that we could "awaken"—areas that we could give more focus on or attention to, areas that we've been neglecting or hiding from, or simply areas that we'd like to rev up. Have you ever had something happen that made you realize you were essentially sleepwalking through that part of your life? A job lost, or an unexpected phone call, or a look in the mirror? Sometimes it occurs to us that we're simply not paying enough attention. To awaken is to regain, or gain for the first time, awareness. To look at the world in wonder or awe. We're going to explore that a bit in this chapter.

Before we dive in, jot down ideas about the category or categories in your life that you might want to awaken. You can circle one from the starter list provided below or write in your own (or both!).

Your mind
Your marriage
Your parenting
Your intimate relationship(s)
Your finances
Your hobbies
Your health and well-being

Your closet

Your spirituality

Your education

Your family

Your friends

Your attitude

Your mindfulness

Your approach to change

Your geographical location

Your spirit

Your heart

Your courage

Your service

Your community

Your traditions

Your makeup

Your skills

Your sports

Your fears

Your public speaking

Your habits

Your inspirations realized

4/18/17

my steps to Completing & publishing my Book.

Next, think of a word that either represents you in some way or that you simply love and are drawn to. Quickly jot down whatever pops into your mind. For example, one of my words is "mischief."

Now create your own drawing of your word. Your drawing can be as elaborate or as simple as you like. Here is my "mischief" drawing:

Begin

Finally, go on an "Awakenings Scavenger Hunt." Give yourself at least thirty minutes to go on a walk or a drive. Try to keep your awakenings topics in mind as you do the following:

- Take at least three pictures. Make sure at least one of them somehow reflects your chosen word. And if you like, go a step further and print them and tape them in your journal.

- Go sit somewhere where there are other people—a coffee shop or another place. Sit, if you can, by a window and spend at least ten minutes just staring out of it, letting your mind go wherever it wants. What came up for you? Write any reflections in your journal.

- Try to find something costing five dollars or less that speaks to your "awaken" topic. Whether you purchase it or not, take a picture of it or write about it.

The Spark

Cup of Golden Sun

I think awakening sometimes begins with appreciation. When my son was two years old, one of his favorite songs to sing was "Do-Re-Mi" from *The Sound of Music*. He would *belt* it, but also get it all mixed up. My favorite adaptation that he made is that he would yell "Ray! A CUP of Golden Sun!"

I mean, why stop at a drop of golden sun when you can have an entire *cup*?

So I started thinking about what it means to have a cup of golden sun in your hands, and the image spoke pretty powerfully to me. I imagined holding this oversized coffee mug that simply glowed as the sunlight spilled out over the top of it. Can you picture it? It made me smile as I started to think about what made up my cup o' sun. What actually made life sunny to me? What made things shine a bit brighter? What didn't I want just a drop of but a whole cup? Here's part of the list that started running through my head:

- My husband
- My kids
- My parents and family
- Flowers
- An unexpected breeze

- A good book
- A glass of wine
- Getting under the cool sheets at the end of a long day
- Driving with the windows down
- The sound of real laughter
- A fountain Diet Coke with extra ice
- Sweet tea
- Pictures of my loved ones, especially when we're making funny faces
- The color yellow
- The big blue sky
- Indiana
- New York City
- The sound of a fiddle or a banjo
- Glitter
- A real hug

It could go on and on. Honestly, the more I thought about my cup of golden sun, the more I realized all that's in it. Soon it would have to be a thermos and eventually a cooler and perhaps even a truckload. When I look for it, it's all around me.

Golden sun, it turns out, expands the more attention you give it. Sure you could stop at a drop-full. A drop-full of sun is a pretty okay thing. But if you invite in a cup-full, soon it will fill every nook and cranny of your day, with things you didn't even realize or expect. Go on; give it a try.

Opportunity for Awakening

What is in your Cup of Golden Sun?

Flip to your journal, set a timer for five minutes, and during that time write down anything that pops into your head that you feel belongs in your cup of golden sun. Try not to think too much; just write down whatever pops in your head. There is nothing too trivial, and there is no reason why something can't show up on your list more than once. Just write, and see what you discover.

The Spark

Overstuffed

Every year we have our annual administrative retreat, wherein we disappear into the woods for a few days and hopefully come out refreshed, reinvigorated, and clearly focused on the goals and plans for the year ahead.

Packing for the trip one year, I was chagrined about how ill-equipped my biggest bag was for the task at hand. A week in the woods needs to include things like sleeping bags and multiple changes of clothes, and if you're at my company, a costume for the annual themed party. I was horrified as I saw the bag grow perilously stuffed before I had even begun to ponder shoes or toiletries—and then I realized that I had actually forgotten to account for an entire *day*.

The end result was a busting-at-the-seams, will-it-make-it-to-New-York sack of ridiculous. I had to leave behind the pack of buckets and shovels I was planning to use for a workshop. And don't get me started on the props and costume pieces that just couldn't make the trip. Sacrifices had to be made.

Something tells me that my bag might perhaps (and only in the remotest possible way, of course) just slightly have resembled my life.

Minus the costumes and buckets, though those certainly play a hearty role in my day to day—both at work and at play—but minus even those, the idea of "stuffing" my life to the gills and overpreparing for every eventuality... well, that rings a bit familiar. Ask anyone who's ever seen my purse. Or my car snack bucket. Or my office inspiration board. Or... well, I think we have enough examples. Let's just say I perhaps overdo it in more ways than just that suitcase debacle. Because I definitely take a "why-have-just-one-when-you-can-have-three?" approach to most things, and that translates into a "why-stop-at-a-nine-to-five-work-day-when-you-can-also-volunteer-to-bring-the-cupcakes-to-the-school-party-and-say-yes-to-the-community-fundraiser" kind of mind-set.

It's a life overstuffed.

And while I LOVE my overstuffed car and bulletin board and suitcase and schedule and life, I also recognize that overstuffed can sometimes end up busting at the seams. Overstuffed can sometimes collapse at the weight of itself. Overstuffed, by definition, means that there is no empty space left. And no empty space means no time, except when sleeping, for rest. No time for contemplation or expansion.

So maybe I didn't need that fourth "just-in-case" shirt in my suitcase for that retreat. And maybe I don't need five varieties of crackers in my car. And maybe I can sometimes say no to an event or opportunity even when the only thing currently on my schedule is... well... nothing. Maybe I can keep a little nothing in my life and allow some "understuffed" time to help balance the overstuffed.

Opportunity for Awakening

What part of your overstuffed life could you unpack a bit today?

Pick a week in the coming month where you are going to practice "unstuffing." During that entire week, say NO to opportunities to socialize, volunteer, take on extra work assignments, or add additional house projects to your weekend. Instead, schedule time in your calendar for nothing. During your nothing blocks, just be, with yourself or whoever is with you—take a walk, read a book, go out for ice cream, sit by the fire, turn on the television. Make your single priority during those nothing blocks to connect with the person/people you are with, whether it is connecting with yourself, your partner, your children, or your friends. See what happens. Keep a log of it in your journal—the date, the time you schedule your "nothing block," and what you ended up doing during that time.

The Spark

No

My kids hate the word "no." For my daughter, hearing "no" when she wants something instantly takes her from an intelligent, witty young girl to a hysterical, weeping, temper-tantrum-throwing sack of crazy. For my son, "no" seems to be one of those words that exist just outside of his sound frequency—he acts as if he actually can't hear it. When he was around two years old, his trick when he wanted to do something that I had said no to was to point his finger at me and say: "Be right back, Mommy. Be right back," as he went to do just the thing I'd told him not to.

Sometimes, when one of my no's has just hurtled the day off course and sent our moods all into a spiral, I find myself thinking, "Why can't they just *listen* to me? Why can't they just $#@*&! go with the flow?"

And then it hits me. I hate the word "no" too.

In fact, "no" is possibly my least favorite word on the planet. If I was on one of those talk shows where they ask you all sorts of questions, and they asked me what word I hate, I'd be hard-pressed to come up with a word I like less than that tiny word. I don't like to be told no in whatever form the no comes in. I don't like to have my own flow blocked. I don't like to be shut down. I find myself immediately resistant to rules simply because they are rules, and that means someone else decided what I can and can't do. I want to do what *I* want to do, because I have good reason to want to do it! (I say, to myself.) I'm truly, genuinely shocked anytime I get in trouble for not following rules—because I would have followed the rules if they *suited* me, but clearly they didn't and therefore I'm making a choice that's better for *me*. "No" is so pesky, it's like a little gnat that I just want to swat away. So, when I hear or feel a no coming my way, I find myself pouting and sulking and generally turning into a teenager (or a toddler), even if only in my head.

Huh.

It occurs to me now that I should probably be more aware of the "me" that is showing up in my kids, whether through genetics or modeling. It also occurs to me that I should possibly consider saying no less and yes more, given that whole karma "you get what you give" kind of thing. If I don't want to hear the no's, why do I think it's okay to so casually *say* the no's?

It further occurs to me that my son was kind of a genius there, and that maybe I should test out his strategy the next time I feel a no coming on. So, I'll just be right back.

Opportunity for Awakening

Are you giving what you want to get?

Practice this "mirror" exercise. In your journal, make two columns. Title the left column "Things That Drive Me Crazy," and in that column write down all the things you can think of that drive you crazy—whether it's the way the slowest drivers always use the left lane or the sound of your coworker eating his sandwich or the fact that your kids always throw their toys on the floor. Then, title the column on the right "Things I Do," and in that column, see if there is any "mirror" of that activity in you—what habits do you have that might be similar to the ones that drive you crazy in others? For example, maybe it drives me crazy when my kids don't clean up their clothes. But then maybe I realize that I often leave my desk a mess at work rather than putting away files.

Once you've done that, reflect back on the two columns. Then, write down any reflections about things you can be more aware of based on any habits you uncovered.

The Spark

I'm Not Worthy

Chaos. Madness. Destruction. Doom and Gloom.

These were the swirling thoughts and emotions that plagued my middle-of-the-night sleeplessness one night, inexplicably tossing me from bad thought to bad thought, leaving me convinced of the utter unworthiness of every. single. thing. I. do.

Okay, maybe it wasn't *that* bad. But it sure felt pretty dismal in the dark hours before dawn. Dark hours where light seemed so very far away, and where the clutches of my evil thoughts were so pervasive they left me paralyzed, unable to simply get up out of bed and literally shake them off, replace them with a snack or some mindless TV, which would have surely lifted my spirits.

I'm not often prone to these middle-of-the-night sessions of "I Suck and So Does My Life And The World And Everything In It," though I know people who battle them pretty regularly. So when I do have a night like that, it leaves me reeling for days and feeling like I'm not worthy.

So often, I think many of us get caught in a "we're not worthy" cycle of thought. It goes back to the whole idea of comparison being a stealer of joy. We compare what we have (or don't have) with what those around us have (or don't have). We compare what we do (or don't do) with what those around us say we should do (or not do). We zero in on our weaknesses and inflate them until there is no room left for us to see anything else. On top of that, we allow ourselves a vicious and completely unhelpful game of "What ifs" that leave us trembling at the thought of the Mights and the Maybes and the Coulds. I don't know about you, but the Mights and the Maybes and the Coulds are scarier monsters than any I've ever worried were lurking under my bed.

Honestly, it's a wonder any of us get out of bed, when you think about it.

On the other hand, while the dust of my sleepless night definitely lingered, tainting everything I looked at with a shade of yuck, it *also* worked to activate the stubborn side of me that refuses to be told how to feel or what to do by anyone, even if it's myself.

It activated the part of me that said, "Dark Night, you will not defeat me!" And so for days afterward, I worked vigorously to actively seek out the light. I looked for the abundance rather than the scarcity. I focused on the goodness instead of the evil. I allowed forced loving thoughts not just toward others but toward myself. I put down my comparison notebook and encouraged myself to just live in the joy. It's pretty cool, this life. And thinking *that* way helps me sleep well at night.

Opportunity for Awakening

What can you do to you remind yourself that you *are* worthy today, even when the "dark night" starts to creep in?

"You ARE Worthy" Ideas:

• Come up with an over-the-top affirmation statement for yourself and write it in your journal. Go a step further and write it with lipstick or crayon on your bathroom mirror. Here's one I've used before, and it's so ridiculous it really works: *"I can only hope my stunning beauty doesn't blind them to my incredible brilliance today."*

• Write mini love notes to yourself on Post-it notes and stick them all around the house.

• Enlist a dear friend to call you at five random times during the course of a week, just to tell you something they love about you.

• Buy yourself flowers, just because.

• What else could you do?

Once you've done one or many of these "You are worthy" ideas, write about the experience in your journal. What was it like?

The Spark

Maybe It's Just Me

So, continuing on a theme of self-criticism.

Maybe it's just me, but sometimes it is quite clear to me that I am the Worst Mom Ever. On these days, I realize with depressing clarity that I am probably a much better parent when I'm not with my children than when I am. Because when I'm not with them, I'm always thinking about them and what I can do to make their life better, happier, more fun, healthier—that's the mom part of me that buys the special treat that I know will make my daughter smile or sets out the toys just the way my son likes them or creates a photo album that they will enjoy at some indefinable point in the future.

But then when I'm *with* them... Do you remember the book *Alexander and the Terrible, Horrible, No Good, Very Bad Day*? Well, that's me, only I'm the one giving my children terrible, horrible, no good, very bad days. I'm the one saying "Do this" and "No, don't do that" and "Hurry up" and "Slow down." I'm the one who just stops paying attention when one of them launches into the fourth crying fit in fifteen minutes.

This happened once when my daughter was four. She and I were having a standoff over dinner—I wanted her to eat *two* bites, and she wanted to eat *zero* bites, but she had gotten candy before dinner, and the deal was she had to eat two bites of dinner, and a deal is a *deal* after all, and so I wasn't budging from my two bite stance, and because she was *four* and she didn't care about *deals* or the importance of dinner for that matter she wasn't budging from *her* stance, and we were at a total impasse. (and blahblahblahblah *blah*! Just telling that story I'm like, "Lady! Just open up a bag of pretzels and move on with the evening already!") ANYWAY. At one point my daughter had run into the other room hysterically crying over what a horrible, mean mother she had. My almost-two-year-old son said to me "Mommy, Marlowe crying." And I said "I know, honey." And he studied me for a beat, then meandered into the other room and I heard him say "What's wrong, Marlowe? What's wrong, Marlowe?" And then it was quiet, and then I heard her giggle a little, so I peeked my head into the room and saw him patting her gently on the back.

And in that moment I was simultaneously struck with horror and wonder. There is nothing more wonderful than to watch my children develop a bond that requires no prompting or cajoling from the outside—it's theirs and theirs alone. And there is hardly a thing more horrible than realizing that, at least in that moment, they were bonding over a common enemy. Me.

Yep. Life can be wonder-full and horror-full all at the same time, can't it?

Opportunity for Awakening

So, maybe it's just me, but do you also sometimes feel like you are the reason for people's no good very bad days?

If NO... Go out and celebrate! Seriously, go get a cake or just stick some candles in whatever food you happen to be eating and keep on loving your wonderful self, because heck YEAH you deserve it.

If YES... Well, come on over and join the Failers' Club, where we fail and fail again. I hope I am not the only member. Here we try to remember that even when life feels horror-full it can also be wonder-full. And wonder-full is not perfect, not by a stretch. In fact, here at the Failers' Club we think the word "perfect" is kind of like the word "unicorn" and most likely only exists in our wonderful imaginations. So pull up a chair. I'll be waiting for you.

And while I'm waiting, take a moment to forgive yourself for all the ways you feel like you failed today, or this week, or this month or year. Forgiveness, especially self-forgiveness, can be hard. Take as long as you need. In your journal, say Dear (insert your name), I forgive you for... and just see what comes up.

The Spark

Roses and Thorns

When my daughter was not-quite five, she and I got into a ridiculous fight over the "rules" of Roses and Thorns.

Roses and Thorns, if you don't know, is a simple activity where you say your "rose" (the best thing) and your "thorn" (the worst thing) for the day. That particular night, while she claimed to be excited to play, when it was my daughter's turn, she declared she didn't have a "rose." I told her that the whole point of the game was to think of one—to find something, anything from the day that made her happy. Well. This threw her into an absolute *fit* as she declared that those were NOT the rules and that you DO NOT have to have a rose. But I wouldn't relent. I told her to think of *any* one moment during the day where she remembered smiling or laughing or having fun or eating something good. After more refusing, pouting, and yelling about how those ARE NOT THE RULES, she sulkily declared that eating macaroni and cheese for lunch was her rose, and that EVERYTHING ELSE IN THE WHOLE DAY was her thorn.

At that moment, she was also refusing to eat her spaghetti because I didn't mix it up right—there had to be noodles on top of the noodles mixed with the meat and the sauce, but the noodles I gave her were the WRONG COLOR. Meanwhile, my then twenty-month-old son had long ago finished his dinner and was tired of being ignored and was shouting ALL DONE! ALL DONE! ALL

DONE! before finally starting to throw his food onto the floor.

As I was on the floor cleaning up his mess, I went back at the Rose and Thorn debate because you know, engaging in a philosophical argument with an almost-five-year-old is usually such a smart thing to do. I was huffily gathering up stray spaghetti noodles and puddles of yogurt and telling her that some days are hard and some days are frustrating and some days the best thing that happens is when I can finally put on my pj's and get ready for BED, but that's okay because at least I found SOMETHING to be grateful about, and that sometimes it is the LEAST WORST THING in your day that becomes your Rose and once again, THAT'S THE WHOLE POINT! when suddenly she hurled herself out of her chair and into my arms. And we hugged. And even my son went quiet for a minute. And I told her that that moment was my new Rose for the day. And I thanked her for sharing her feelings with me. And all was well.

Until fifteen minutes later when she got in trouble for shoving her brother onto the floor (after he had gotten in trouble for pulling her hair).

When the Roses are in full bloom, they're easy to spot. But on days where they're hidden quite well underneath the thorns, it's often when they're most important to find. And if you look closely enough, if you push the thorns gently aside, you can always find one. Even if it's just that you made it to bedtime.

Opportunity for Awakening

Where can you find your Rose today?

Spend the day seeking your "roses." When you find them, give
something to the person/situation that is creating the rose
for you—a thank-you, a hug, a literal flower, however you can
acknowledge it outwardly and in the moment. Spread "roses"
throughout the day.

How was your day? Write about it in your journal.

The Spark

The Moments That We Remember

I've been thinking about those moments that either subtly or profoundly affect the way we interact with the world.

Some of those moments are earth-shattering, like the first time Loss comes up and punches you squarely in the face (*for me, that came in the form of a 7:00 a.m. phone call when I was seventeen years old, alerting me to the death of one of my most beloveds*).

Some of those moments are seemingly trivial, like the first time you find your own unique style (*I still remember trying to explain to my mom just how important grunge music was as a college student in the early '90s*).

Sometimes those moments change the very face of the world, like the first time you encounter a national or global crisis (*Nothing will soften the memory of standing on a rooftop in Manhattan with some of my coworkers, some blocks north of the World Trade Center, marveling at the gaping holes in the sides of the buildings, when the sudden, distant rumble of some kind of thunder preceded the slow and shocking collapse of the first tower*).

Sometimes those moments make you aware that you've never actually understood the full function of your heart until then (*While I thought my elementary-age heart fully opened up when I first saw* Stand By Me *and was introduced to the glory of River Phoenix, it was actually the first time I held my first baby that*

I knew the world would forever be so much more terrifying, heartbreaking, beautiful, wide open and exquisite, and that I could never hide my heart from any of it again).

Sometimes those moments show us just how important our voice actually is (*I spent the first year and a half at The Leadership Program waiting for an invitation to be included, to be liked, to be considered worthy. And then I got tired of waiting and just declared myself included... and I've now spent more than sixteen years declaring rather than waiting*).

And some of those moments aren't actual moments at all, but rather the accumulation of pieces of moments that you suddenly become aware of on a random Tuesday (*like clinking coffee mugs across the table with my husband and suddenly being hit with the profound weight of the remarkable life we've created together, side by side, interwoven in ways that are not explainable and that extend so far past the pictures on the wall of two young people on their wedding day, practically strangers to me now*).

Whether small (*How did I ever live in a world without minivans?*) or big (*This wide-open heart thing that my children have created in me is sometimes unbearable*), these are the moments that offer an opportunity for something to stir in us. It's as if one of the many layers that color how we view the world gets peeled away, and as such the color shifts just a bit and the world looks different, forever.

Opportunity for Awakening

What are the moments you remember?

Whether small or big, what are the moments that have stirred
something in you, either temporarily or permanently? Take
some time in your journal and allow yourself to sift through your
memories and find those moments.

The Spark

On Awakening

What does it actually mean to awaken? One of the definitions that I love has it as "to spring into being."

I don't know about you, but when I wake up each morning, I spend some amount of time in that foggy space between sleep and awakening. That space in which my body refuses to cooperate and my mind tries to grasp at the details of the day ahead, all while my eyes stay stubbornly shut in rebellion of it all. It can feel like a treacherous uphill trudge, the awakening. And I usually spend no small amount of time wishing myself backward—back into the world of sleep, where I was just so comfortable.

But when I get there, when I finally do spring into being, the *day* becomes what I want, not the sleep.

I really do think the same is true when we're trying to awaken anything—it can be a treacherous uphill trudge to get there. It can be tempting to skip it altogether—but if we skip it, we miss out on the possibilities of what lies ahead. We miss out on the *day*.

Now, to be fair, of course there are bad days. Days where awakening turns out to be a cruel joke, and the comfort of sleep really IS what we want to run back to as fast as we can. Awakening doesn't always go our way. And on those days, maybe going back to sleep—resetting—really is the best thing to do. But the next day gives us another chance to awaken, another chance to try, another chance just to see what's possible.

So whether you are trying to awaken your marriage or your career or your courage; whether you are trying to awaken a long-lost hobby or a desire for travel; whether you are trying to awaken your finances or your closet, remember that while the comfort of *not* awakening can be oh so cozy, the joy of awakening can be oh so much more. It may be layered and complex, it may have stops and starts, it may be different than you thought. It may even make you turn to another direction. All that awakening can be messy and vulnerable and hard. But how much richer life is when we strive to awaken! So go ahead, throw off the covers. Put your feet on the floor. Who knows what awaits you.

Opportunity for Awakening

Once awakened, how can you *stay* awake?

Look back at your word, the one that you wrote at the beginning of this chapter. Write it again in your journal or right here in this book, as big as you can. Now surround your word with other words, thoughts, quotes, phrases, images, or pictures that represent awakening to you.

Next, take a moment to look back at all your notes from the "Awaken" chapter, and jot down any discoveries you've made, or any thoughts you want to hold on to. Next, we're on to "Unfolding"!

Chapter Two: Unfold

Overview

So, we started with "Awaken," which was designed to awaken thoughts or feelings in you, perhaps create a fresh awareness about something, or some things. In this chapter, we're moving on to the theme of "Unfolding." I think it's a good idea to expand our exploration into what we believe, feel, and think, challenging even further our perspectives and assumptions. Thus, we will start to unfold more deeply the topics we've been thinking about. To unfold means to reveal, or lay open to view. To unfold means to go beyond just being awake; to unfold means to uncover. And hopefully, in the course of this unfolding, you just might discover, or rediscover, some things that are wow-worthy about your life.

Before we dive in, take a field trip to your local library or book store. Instead of going straight for the self-help section or the books on business leadership, take a turn to the children's section. Yes! The children's section! I've come to believe that some of the best advice for work and life comes from these shelves, and I'd love to see what you think about that theory. So I've offered four children's books here for you to read and offer your response to, and of course you should feel free to discover lessons from another children's book as well. Have fun!

- *Harold and the Purple Crayon*, by Crockett Johnson

- *Scaredy Squirrel*, by Melanie Watt

- *Not a Box*, by Antoinette Portis

- *I Like Myself*, by Karen Beaumont

Read one or all of them and then write any thoughts or responses about them in your journal, as well as what, if anything, you think they have to do with the idea of "unfolding."

The Spark

New Year

I've never much been a fan of New Year's resolutions. I think this is partly because I am a very sedentary person by nature and do not like to exert myself in unpleasant things like going to the gym or cleaning the house, and partly because I generally don't like to be told what to do, even if it's just me telling myself what to do.

Because things start and stop, don't they? We declare that this is the year we will exercise three days a week, and so we buy a cute outfit and an expensive gym membership, and go to the gym *four* days in that first week just to prove how new and improved we are. But then. But then. But then the kids get the flu, and the work deadline consumes more of our time than expected, and our back hurts, and our friend suggests we go to a movie, and frankly we'd rather eat nachos and watch our favorite TV show—or just go to sleep already—and before we know it we're going to the gym three times a *year* rather than three times a week. And then the year comes to an end and we say "well that was a massive fail, wasn't it?"

I don't know about you, but I just don't find that to be very motivating.

Instead, I'd rather think of all that as just life. We start and stop, and start and stop again. I am constantly trying to catch up with my gray hair and my Amex bill. I clean the house from top to bottom and declare I will never let it get messy again, and then within two days it's back to looking like something from the show *Hoarders*. I remember one friend's very important occasion, but then completely forget a family member's birthday. I say okay to "staying up all night" on New Year's Eve, but then say no to playing in the snow. I am awesome and then I am horrible; I am incredibly smart and then shockingly shortsighted; I am skinny and then I am well cushioned. I am loving and then completely rude. I am so very simple and straightforward and also incredibly complex.

So I can sit here and add up my deficits versus my benefits, but we all know how those lists work out for us. Or I can just say: How beautiful. How beautiful to be *all this* in the year that has just passed.

Yes, I think I would rather celebrate the year that has just been completed—the highs and lows, the funny, the sad, the hard, the beautiful. And then I would rather approach the new year with an open heart and mind, without expectations, lists, and judgments. Focusing on scarcity is just too easy; I would rather focus on abundance. I would rather. Of course, if I spend too much time on *this* line of thinking, I might start to believe keeping a nightly gratitude journal is the thing for me, and then I'm right back to the whole resolution problem.

And anyway, expecting to fully embrace the year with an open heart and a focus on abundance is just as difficult as expecting to finally fill in the blank.

Consider this scene in my house one night:

Before dinner, my then four-year-old daughter decided to strip down to just her underwear and her necklace with the very large heart pendant. My then twenty-month-old son thought that since his sister wasn't wearing a shirt, he shouldn't either. Together, half-naked, the two of them laughed and danced and jumped around the kitchen to some ridiculous pop song. *Love.* Fast forward five minutes to when both were hysterically crying because there was only ONE CUP in the entire house that either of them was willing to drink their water from, and my son had gotten to it first. *Horror.* Fast forward to bath-time when, as I was filling the bathtub, I could see that in my daughter's bedroom my son was gleefully banging my husband over the head with a toy hair dryer while my daughter was playing contentedly with her dollhouse. *Love.* Fast forward to one o'clock in the morning when my son was awake and refusing to go into his crib, shouting "No! Out!" every time I tried to lay him down. *Horror.* Fast forward to two o'clock in the morning when we finally just lay down together in our guest room, both of us tangled up together and finally sleeping. *Love.* (Well, that is until I woke up the next morning to discover he had peed all over both of us.)

I use the story of that night as a small example of why I believe we have such a hard time keeping resolutions in the end. We paint a picture of what our lives should look like based on the pictures we see of other lives, but pictures capture moments, not lives. And our lives are made up of a million moments a day, both love moments and horror moments and plenty of "eh" moments in between.

Life goes on. The best we can do is simply show up, try our best, try again, forgive ourselves, forgive others, enjoy the love moments, remember that the horror moments won't last forever, laugh as much as possible, and remind ourselves that perfection is an illusion.

Opportunity for Unfolding

Whether you are literally at the new year, or just newly looking at the year you're currently in: How can you just *be* here for it?

Find twenty minutes to sit and reflect on this year so far. Write down all that has happened that you can remember—the love moments, the horror moments, the eh moments, and everything in between. When you are done, I invite you to go one step further and go get a flower or another object from nature that could be pressed between the pages. Why nature? I think it's easy to get so caught up in the motions of our days that we forget our connection to the universe. So, grab a small piece of the universe, say a word of gratitude for all that has been a part of your year.

The Spark

The "All" of It All

So often I try to "do it all" in the most overused, traditional doing-it-all way: I try to act as both a stay-at-home mom and a full-time-working mom.

For those of you who are thinking "Hey, Einstein—the laws of physics and gravity and the time/space continuum actually prevent that from being possible." Well. Yes. Apparently you are right.

Many weeks start off innocently enough—with a few planned doctor appointments and volunteer obligations at my daughter's school, carefully scheduled throughout an already busy work week of meetings and presentations. But then a myriad of *unscheduled* things undoubtedly occur, like sickness (which mean more doctor appointments). And snow days. And unexpected deadlines. And broken printers. As a result, I spend much of those weeks running around in crazy circles and frequently shouting exclamations like "$#@$*&!!!!!!!"

Other weeks start off crazy to begin with, like this one: I'm trying to be prepared for a third week of work travel in a row. I'm trying to contribute to the many Parent Teacher Organization opportunities. I'm trying to keep up with the house, which is laughable. Two weekends in a row of yard work have left the floors and surfaces smeared with dirt that I am too tired to mop up. Bags from a trip to the store three days ago have been forgotten on the floor. Bags from my last week of travel are yet unpacked, making packing for this week's travel difficult. I'm trying to prepare for the weekend ahead, which contains a beautiful explosion of celebrations. I'm trying to keep up with this week's laundry even though last week's laundry is still not put away. I'm trying to tackle my inbox, which is teetering dangerously close to neglect. And is that a scratch in my throat? I'm trying to be mindful of checking in on my friends who so desperately need checking in on during extraordinarily difficult times. I'm trying to figure out how to fix the stinkin' TV when it's bedtime and the kids just HAVE to watch their usual bedtime shows and the satellite goes out. I'm trying to fit a shower in. I'm trying to follow up with the insurance, drop off the casserole for the neighbors with the new baby, finish the overdue report, fix the broken bike, tend to my sort-of-sick daughter, get situated for next week's *fourth* week in a row of travel, and do my nails which are ragged and mulch stained.

So whether the weeks start off innocently or start off crazy, I'm trying to keep it all in the air, to keep it all handled, to do every part of it, and do it well. But trying to do it all is not only treacherous, it's impossible. There will never be a time when I stand proudly on top of my mountain of "all" and declare it conquered. Instead I will continue to look at up at that mountain from a place that feels far, far away—so far away that I have to strain my neck to see the top—and I will gulp in nervous anticipation of how to proceed.

At least I hope I do.

For when I look at the "all" before me, all I can really think is this: how blessed am I? How blessed to be able to have to deal with all of those things, and more? How delightful to be given so much to tackle? How rich, how full, how beautiful this chaotic and messy life is.

So, to my list and beyond, I say: Here I come! I'm climbing up that mountain, one "all" at a time. I'll do some of it well and some of it sort of okay and some of it terribly. But I will keep at it, every day. I will show up, arms wide open, gloriously trying. And, in the end, I think that's good enough for me.

Because on those starting-off-innocently weeks or those starting-off-crazy weeks, when it's 5:00 a.m., and the spring birds are in full symphony to awaken the day, and I have a huge mug of steaming coffee next to me, and the house is quiet save the creaks and groans of the walls and floors that contain so much beautiful chaos, and my sort-of-sick daughter and my oh-then-I-must-be-sick-too son are curled up together in my bed, probably with at least one foot or hand squarely in my wonderful husband's face, well, all I can think to say is *thank you.*

Opportunity for Unfolding

How can you embrace the "all" in your life?

What's on your to-do list? For three minutes, write everything that pops into your mind—work to-dos, family to-dos, personal to-dos, way overdue to-dos—include it all.

Take a look at the list you've created. Take a few deep breaths in, and with every exhale, offer a quiet thank-you for the opportunities before you. Now stop looking at the whole list, and just look at one thing on the list. Just do one thing. When that thing is done, pick another—one to-do at a time; that's how the world is conquered, I tell you.

The Spark

Housekeeping

I don't know how people keep a nice house, *ever.*

My house is never ready for surprise visitors, as it is hardly suitable for those of us who live in it. There are tumbleweeds of dust floating down the hallway. There are layers of generic kid-slime on the coffee table. There are toys everywhere. There is unfolded laundry in the laundry room and the bedrooms. The beds are unmade. There is scum in the bathtub, and there are dishes in the sink. There are piles of unopened mail. And don't even get me started on the basement. (Where I work. Every day!)

I *try* to find time to do the cleaning. I even try to make schedules so that I just have to tackle it in small bits and parts. Some days I arm myself with more than a box of Clorox Wipes, and declare battle with this house. A sparkling house with sparkling windows (really, you need to clean *both sides* of the windows?) and sparkling floors and toys perfectly placed in every perfect container. Fresh flowers on the table and a healthy dinner cooking in the oven. On those days, it is a picture of healthy, clean perfection, at least for a moment.

Because then the kids come home and real life begins again. Life that involves so much more than just me alone with my bucket of cleaning supplies. Life that involves snacks and games and paint. Life that says, "yes, the blinds need to be dusted, but your daughter currently wants her face dusted with fairy glitter." Life that says, "yes those toys should be put away, but your son wouldn't be able to build a train out of a book, a chair, a toy guitar, a set of Legos, a pillow, and a fire truck if everything was put away, now would he?"

So while the house often reminds me that I need to probably pay a bit more attention to the floorboards and the cobwebs, and that we should probably put something away *sometime*, my children perpetually remind me that, in the end, that's not what matters the most.

Opportunity for Unfolding

Do you have blinds that need dusting *and* faces that need to be dusted with fairy glitter? How can you balance your obligations with your opportunities today?

Take pictures of your favorite parts of your home, your favorite things within your home, and the place in your home that you/your family/your friends spend the most time. Don't clean up those spaces before you take the pictures. Paste them in your journal, and next to each picture, write a story about something that has happened in that space that has made you laugh or smile.

The Spark

Life

A dear friend of mine once went through a crisis that was heartbreaking. It was the kind of crisis that leaves the rest of us helplessly asking if we can bring snacks.

There are many kinds of crises in our lives. There are the kinds that happen unexpectedly; there are the kinds that aren't really that bad but that we turn into a big deal; there are the ones that happen entirely in our own minds without any help from the real world (I'm especially good at those). And then there are the ones like my friend was facing—those ones that seek to shatter all that we take comfort in. But all crises take a toll, and often leave us pondering the meaning of life and all that is in it: How stunningly fragile it is. How stunningly beautiful and how stunningly hard. It is in these moments that I, like many of you, start to remind myself not to take a single day for granted, to be present and grateful for every moment, to laugh with my kids and not be impatient, to let go of the things that are weighing me down.

The thing about that, though, is that it is all very *hard* to do in real life.

Because here is what happens:

I will sit down with my kids and declare myself *present* and ready to laugh and play, but then five minutes into that, one of them will hit the other or start to throw a fit and all the sunshine and magic will disappear and we will once again just be our messy grumpy selves.

I will tell myself to see the beauty in every moment, and then I will go out to shovel the five-hundredth snow of the season, and I will DECLARE IT BEAUTIFUL, and I will see the fresh snow sparkling like diamonds, and I will laugh at how the falling snow makes me feel like I am in a snow globe, and I will breathe in the crisp air and feel all the muscles in my body working to shovel the snow. And then the city snow plow will drive by and dump three feet of street snow at the end of my freshly shoveled driveway. And then I will wake up the next morning with an aching back that won't go away for a month.

I will declare myself free of all the things that are worrying my mind, but then my mind will ignore my declaration and wake me up at 3:00 a.m. to go ahead and worry anyway. And, while it's worrying, it will dredge up some twenty-year-old wound for me to reminisce about too. Because, you know, that's always helpful.

I will know in my head and in my heart that this day is precious, that this day is the only day I have, but I will still curse at the food that spills on the floor, and the computer that takes too long to load, and the phone call I don't want to take, and the dinner I have to figure out even though the fridge is lacking anything proper. I will spend too much time on some Facebook post that I don't even care about and not enough time on the family that I do.

Because THIS is life. Life is happy and grumpy, messy and clean, appreciative and bitter, tearful and funny. It is petty annoyances and earth-shattering moments. It is coffee and it is cathedrals. Sometimes life is long and sometimes life is much, much too short. Life is an ocean of everything—the things we take for granted and the things we remember to love fiercely. The things we notice and the things we lose sight of. It's amazing, this life. Every part of it. So rather than berating myself for not appreciating it more, for not doing it "better," instead I am just going to look around at the "everything" of it and just take a moment to say WOW.

Opportunity for Unfolding

How can you say WOW today?

Now that you've taken some pictures of what's wow-worthy in your house, it's time to find the "wow" that's around you. So, go on a thirty-minute walk. Take your camera with you. Leave your phone behind (unless your phone *is* your camera, in which case just turn it on airplane mode so you'll be free from calls, pop-ups, and alerts) and keep your ears free from earbuds that would distract you with music or books. Just walk, absorb the sights you see and the sounds you hear. Try and stay focused on the present moment, and use that focus to notice things you've never noticed before. Take pictures along your entire walk. Later, print the pictures and paste them in your journal. Next to the pictures, write down your thoughts on the things that make you go WOW.

The Spark

Changing Landscapes

Once, in my early twenties, I rear-ended a city bus. During the busy morning commute. A city bus filled with passengers. Passengers who all had to evacuate the bus upon my rear-ending of it and wait on the sidewalk for a new bus. Passengers who waited while glaring silently, or not so silently, at me, as I also waited for the police and the insurance and the blah blah blah that follows such an event. One woman said to me incredulously "Why did you *do* that?" Why, indeed.

Now, in my defense...

It was at the height of the steady humming morning commute. I had stopped to get gas. Pulling out of the gas station, I had to make a right and then immediately get over in the far left lane to make a left at the stoplight just a hundred feet or so away. This was a busy three-lane road, so I was poised to make my right turn out of the gas station at precisely the moment that I could get across all three lanes simultaneously. Are you with me? So, I was poised to turn right, but I was looking left. Looking, looking, looking, for my moment. As I waited and looked, a city bus passed in front of me. I registered this fact, but didn't *register* it. Because right after that, I got my moment. All lanes were clear, traffic was moving, and so I gunned it out of the gas station and straight into the city bus. The city bus that, once it had passed me, had promptly stopped at the bus stop located right in front of the gas station.

So, incredulous lady who wondered aloud just why I did that. I did that because I had a clear plan of action that made sense if all traffic flowed as I assumed, expected, and thought it would; if it kept going the way it had been going. I did that because I was so confident in my plan that I looked left while I was turning right and didn't think to check the landscape and make sure nothing had changed before I started to move. I did that because I didn't count on the bus.

I didn't count on the bus.

Maybe you've had such a moment, too. Hopefully it hasn't involved a busload of people glaring at you in the middle of a busy street. But a moment where you had a plan—a plan that would work if everything went as it was supposed to, if everyone involved moved where they were supposed to, did what they were supposed to, said what they were supposed to. A plan that went disastrously wrong because someone or something did not actually do what they were "supposed to" at all, and because you didn't check the landscape to notice the changes. A plan that went wrong because you didn't change it to accommodate what was actually happening rather than what you *wanted* to happen.

If I had only looked right, just once, before entering traffic that day, I would have seen that my plan needed to change, that the bus had changed the landscape. If I had looked right, I would have made the changes that would have allowed for: me getting to my scheduled destination unshaken and on time, the people on the bus having a completely uninterrupted (albeit much more boring) ride without any delays to their day, and my car (and ego) not being a bit smooshed.

Opportunity for Unfolding

Are you looking out for the landscape changes ahead?

Think about a time where the landscape changed in front of you and you didn't adjust for it. Maybe you realized that you didn't actually want to be an engineer as you were walking across the stage to collect your diploma celebrating your degree in engineering. Maybe you kept getting together with a group of old friends long after you realized that you didn't agree with most of the things they talked about. Maybe you kept pushing an idea forward at work long after it became clear that no one on your team was interested in it. Maybe you kept going to the same store even after the service was terrible every single time. Maybe you forced your daughter to have a birthday party at the local bounce house because that's where all the kids were going, even though she really wanted to just stay home. Maybe you held on to a pair of pants that haven't fit you for fifteen years, just in case this was the year they did.

Maybe you're still doing those things.

Write your thoughts about the times when the landscape in front of you has changed and you haven't. How has that affected you, positively or negatively? What might have been different in those moments if you had adjusted to the changing landscape?

The Spark

The Block

Writer's block is a horrible thing. I write a blog every Tuesday, and many a Monday-into-Tuesday I stare at the computer screen without an inkling of an idea of what to write for it. I stare at a blank page, desperately searching the deepest vaults of my brain, searching for anything remotely interesting to say, while that blank page taunts me menacingly with its glaring blankness. On those days, I become convinced that the gig is up—that my time of pretending to be a viable content creator is done, that I shouldn't have thought I could keep this up, anyway. I mean, who am *I* after all? It's all quite depressing, really.

And then something sparks. Sometimes it starts as the tiniest flicker of far off light; sometimes it hits me like lightning. A memory, something funny the kids do, a story from work, a gripping bit of breaking news. And within that spark I find the beginning. And once I find the beginning, I usually get a hold of the thread that will carry me through to the end. Every week this happens, yet every week before the spark comes I doubt its very existence.

It's the "I can't do it!" cycle that grips so many of us at the start of something—when we are at the start of a project, at the eve of the deadline, at the edge of the cliff. Our self-doubt can be crippling just before we cross over that line, just before we begin. I don't know why it continues to happen to me—each and every time I work myself up into a state of "I'm A Total Idiot," yet each and every time I remember that the spark *will* come. You'd think by now I'd be able to stop the fear and the doubt. But no. Because the insecurity is continuously stronger than the belief. The loudest and most persuasive voice in my brain is inevitably the one yelling at me that I *can't*, rather than the one whispering to me that I probably actually *can*.

Does this happen to you? Do you get the new job and then worry that you'll be discovered a fraud? Do you buy the sassy new outfit and then spend the entire day convinced people are judging your choice? Do you have to spend minutes (or hours) working up the courage to pick up the phone for a call you really wish to make? Do you sign up for a class and then stay home because you're convinced you'll be the oldest one there?

Today look for a reminder—they are all around you—that "I can't" is really an invented stopping point; a voice in our brain, not an absolute truth.

Opportunity for Unfolding

What "I can't do it" voice inside your head can you squelch today, by just going ahead and doing it anyway?

Pick a day where you're going to try and do something you think you "can't" do—whether it's making a phone call, singing karaoke, running in a race, taking a class, asking for a loan, writing a story— whatever it is. Pick your day, and write it in your calendar. Write it in your journal. Write it right here too. (And probably tell a close friend about it so you have some extra support.) Write the date and the thing you're going to do, and then once you've finished, write about your experience in your journal.

The Spark

Shark Attack

My mom and I once almost got attacked by a shark, sort of.

We were on vacation in Panama City, Florida. She and I were sitting about twenty feet out in the ocean, facing the beach. We were in the warm, shallow water, leisurely chatting, when a few things caught our attention. First, there was a small crowd of people on the beach, waving at us. Second, we appeared to be the only ones in the water. Third, the people waving at us were also talking to us. We started to tune in more closely and discovered that the waving people would be better described as "gesturing wildly" people, and the things they were saying to us included words like "Shark!" and "Get out of the water!"

Now. One thing that people who know me know about me is this: number ONE on my list of Things That Scare the Pee Right Out of Me is, in fact, sharks.

So, the realization that wildly gesturing people were using the word "shark" to my mom and me while we were very solidly *in the water* was very troubling indeed.

Naturally I did what every good daughter who loves her mother would do—I shoved her out of my way and started water-running my way toward the beach. She, meanwhile, did what every mother in the universe would do—she placed herself solidly behind me so that shark would get her first.

Have you ever tried to run in water, particularly sandy water? It's like those nightmares where you try to run, but you're moving in slow motion—there is simply *no way* to do it fast. So I was sluggishly water-running my way toward the beach, watching the wildly gesturing people add some new words to their repertoire, like "It's right behind you!" I just knew that horrifying death was imminent.

And then I made it to the beach. And I looked behind me to discover that my mom, too, had made it to the beach (no thanks to me). And then the two of us looked out at the water to view the shark that had caused such panic on the beach. It took our eyes a moment, but we were able to discern a long gray shadow moving in the water. We, along with our wildly gesturing people, watched the shadow come closer, close enough for us to get a good look. And we discovered that our shark was actually a group of stingrays swimming together.

Things are not always what they seem. The shark turns out to just be a bunch of stingrays playing in the water. The aggressive behavior of a friend or coworker turns out to be an attempt to hide feelings of fear or confusion. The problem that seems ALL CONSUMING in the middle of the night turns out to be, when faced in the light of day, just not that big a deal. Sometimes you just need to look twice.

Opportunity for Unfolding

Are there any "sharks" chasing you?

Are there any "sharks" chasing you? Whether in the form of people or problems, turn around and face them. Ask them questions. Are they what they appear to be or is there more to the story? Record your observations in your journal—what was the "shark" and what did you think it was? Did that end up being the full truth, or was there more to the story? How often were your thoughts about the "shark" exactly accurate? Did any common themes emerge? What, if anything, did you discover from facing your "sharks"?

The Spark

On Failing

Sometimes you fail at work.

Sometimes, it's a loud and epic fail—like losing your company millions of dollars or insulting your biggest client or spearheading a product that flops. Those definitely suck, and sometimes cost you your job or your reputation.

But sometimes—and I think more often—the failure is much quieter. Sometimes, you fail to understand the importance of an issue with a coworker. Sometimes, you fail to communicate a need properly. Sometimes, you fail to listen.

I fail *all the time* at work. I've occasionally had the big loud flopper fails, but most often, I fail in the quiet ones. I go through phases where I feel like I have one failure after the other, with times where my failure hits me square in my face as I watch the disappointment in the face of another.

These are the failures you feel in your gut.

The thing I've noticed about those failures is they usually start with me becoming Very Defensive and Sure of My Rightness. As I get older, I am starting to realize that defensiveness is usually a clue that I'm actually quite wrong. Defensiveness is just my body's initial fight against the inevitable need to confess that I messed up or that I don't know or that I need help. And if I can identify that quickly and let my defensiveness go, then I can get to the apologizing and fixing much faster. Usually this plays out in the middle of the night. The 3:00 a.m. restlessness where I have an inner fight in my mind, debating the half of my brain that Firmly Declares that I've Done Nothing Wrong with the half of my brain that urges me to Give It Up Already, You Know You Screwed Up.

I know that the hardest part about failing, for me, is the *feeling* that goes with it, more than the actual failure itself—it's the feeling of guilt, the feeling of I'm A Horrible Person and Not Deserving of Love. This is ironic because when I feel that I've been failed by someone else, I usually love them much more if they can just confess to screwing up—confess to being human and flawed. Why is it that we appreciate the humanity in others but try so hard to hide it in ourselves?

I have to go now. I owe a coworker (or three) an apology.

Opportunity for Unfolding

How can you own up to a quiet failure today?

Think of the people in your life—your family, your coworkers, your neighbors, your friends, your community. Is there anyone whom you might have failed recently? Go talk to them about it.

After you do... How did it go? Write about it in your journal.

The Spark

On Unfolding

The idea of unfolding means many things; some of my favorites from the dictionary include: *to bring out of a folded state; to spread out or lay open to view; to reveal or display; to become unfolded or open; to develop; to become clear, apparent, or known.*

Unfolding, then, becomes about revealing something—a discovery, perhaps. A part of yourself previously left hidden. A new talent. A new direction. Whatever it is, this unfolding, most likely involves a vulnerability and exposure. And that can be very uncomfortable, especially at first. Made even more so by the fact that sometimes our unfolding leads to discoveries we don't like. Or decisions that don't work out. But the possibilities!

Think of it like unwrapping a present, this unfolding. As you peel back the wrapping paper, and get a first glimpse of what lies underneath, isn't the anticipation glorious? And as you further unwrap the present to fully discover what lies underneath, sometimes you'll be met with the dull disappointment of yet another pair of socks, sometimes you'll be met with the "eh" of a book of car wash coupons. But *sometimes,* oh, sometimes... Sometimes what lies beneath that wrapping paper takes your breath away. Sometimes it is exactly what you wished for. Sometimes it's something you never knew you wanted but soon can't imagine ever living without. Sometimes it's a gift of love so overwhelming it brings you to tears. You'll never know if you don't unwrap the paper.

And so it goes with our lives—we can leave them wrapped up tight and probably be just fine. Or we can begin to peel back the layers and see what happens. I don't know about you, but the prospect of the discovery to be found in the unwrapping is just too tempting to pass up.

Opportunity for Unfolding

Take a look back at your notes from the children's books that
started this chapter. Maybe even reread a few of the books,
or take another trip to the children's aisle and see what you
discover. Did anything come up for you when reading the books?
Then, reflect back on your notes from the "Unfolding" chapter
and highlight anything that stands out for you. What parts were
difficult—or what things did you avoid all together? What themes
emerged, if any? When you're ready to move on, we're heading
over to "Illuminate."

Chapter Three:
Illuminate

Overview

So, we've awakened and we've unfolded, and now it's time to illuminate. What is illumination? Illumination means to "throw light on" something. While the "unfolding" section hopefully gave you some moments of scratching your head and saying "huh," the "illuminating" section is designed to hopefully offer some moments of "ah!"

Before we dive in, think about some of the areas you've been gravitating toward in the awakening and unfolding sections. Next, identify three people in your life who, from your perspective, "do" that thing, or those things, really well. For example, if one of your areas of awakening is to advance your financial situation, you might talk to a friend who seems to be in excellent financial shape. Ask them if they would be willing to talk to you about that topic area, and think about at least five questions you'd like to ask them on the topic. Write your questions, and their answers, in your journal.

Once you've finished, reflect on the experience:

• Did anything surprise you about any of your interview responses?

• What reflections do you have upon the conclusion of the interviews?

• Did you gain any tools or action steps to help you move forward?

The Spark

Beautiful

By the time my daughter was three years old, she had already acquired an awareness of a well-known horror: the mean girl.

At her preschool, there was one girl in particular who really got under her skin. Nearly every night she'd recount some mean thing this girl had said or done. I remember one conversation in particular that went something like this:

Her: Mommy, XX told me that I wasn't beautiful.

Me: What? Of course you're beautiful. Just don't pay her any attention.

Her: Yeah, and she told me I was nothing.

Me (*after a few moments of silent, immature thoughts of just what my response could be to that young girl*): What do you mean, she said "you were nothing?"

Her: We were playing "family" and she said I wasn't anything—not the mommy or the baby or anything.

Oh. Okay.

But still.

Already, at just three, these young girls and boys were aware of how others can tell us how to feel about ourselves. As adults we know this too well, don't we? Tell me ten fantastic things you think about me and I'll shrug them away, but toss a sarcastic comment or stinging bit of criticism my way and I'll carry it heavily for days.

I remember when research professor Brené Brown first came into the public arena and I listened to her amazing TED talks in which she spoke about vulnerability, shame, and courage. She talked about courage as being the ability to *tell the story of who you are with your own heart.* I thought that was so beautiful—in the face of everything else, can you tell the story of who you are with your own heart, rather than with the voices of others?

As adults this is hard enough to do. So, imagine our young people. Just think of the battles they must be waging in their own minds against the voices of those who are telling them that they are not beautiful, that they are nothing. And so, while we can't completely stop the tide of negative messages that people receive, we can certainly ensure that those aren't the *only* messages they are receiving. Because we are all beautiful, in our own way, no? Sometimes we just need a little help remembering it—a little help to find the courage to tell the story of who we are with our own heart.

The most important thing I can do for my children is to remind them that I think they are the most beautiful, smart, creative, funny, clever people I know. I can also teach them—through my own actions—how to walk away from the negativity; how to say "that is not true for me" in response to those zingers, those stingers, those words that do, in fact, hurt—sometimes more than sticks and stones. And I can remember to do that for myself too.

Opportunity for Illumination

Whose beauty can you highlight today?

One Day Challenge: Pick one day where you find some way
to compliment _____ people you encounter. You pick the
number to fill in the blank—One? Ten? Every single person who
crosses your path? Your choice! When you've finished, write some
reflections on how it went in your journal.

The Spark

Love Is a Verb

When I love you, it's really easy to love you. But when you do things that make me *not* love you, well then it's really hard to love you.

I mean, *obviously.*

List the people in your life for whom that sentiment rings true from time to time—a partner, a coworker, a child, a friend. Your football team.

I don't know about you, but I know that I can easily get caught up in the lists of things that aren't happening, that aren't going right, that aren't unfolding the exact way I think they should, and in doing so become clouded to the fact that the faces behind those lists belong to people who are—just like me—probably doing the best they can.

My boss once led us in a workshop where she talked about the "rocks" we accumulate throughout any given day—the baggage we collect when things don't go our way or when we perceive that someone has wronged us.

Using literal rocks to demonstrate, she showed us how heavy and weighed down we can become when we hold onto every perceived annoyance, disappointment, misunderstanding, or gripe—when each of those becomes a rock we add to our pockets. If we hold onto all of those rocks, it doesn't take long to become very heavy indeed. And if we take those rocks home with us, and if we don't find a way to put them down, we start every new day already heavy with the rocks from the day before. You can see how quickly the rocks can become all we feel.

Love, in its most powerful sense, is a verb. It's not simply a thing to receive, and it's also not simply a thing we bestow upon those that are "worthy." Instead, it's a choice we make in the way we approach the people with whom we interact. All of them. Even (and especially) when it's not easy.

So what happens when I make the choice to put down all my rocks and actively love the heck out of everyone in my path? I'm not exactly sure, but I imagine it quite possibly means I have to stop yelling at the Colts if they happen to be in a losing streak, as if it is something they are doing to me personally. And I suppose it also means I have to actually have a conversation face-to-face with the coworker rather than just pouting and grumbling off to the side. And I guess it further means that I need to just be at peace with the fact that yes, I am going to have to tell my son yet *again* not to hit me, or his sister, because the fact is that he's trying to figure out how to express himself when his brain and his body aren't in sync.

Love as a verb is much more difficult than love as a gift. In fact, thinking about it makes me kind of want to say, "It's okay; I'll just grab all my rocks and go, thank you very much." But if we embrace that approach, if it informs every interaction, then the possibility for connection and understanding is so much richer. And how much *lighter* we feel when we're not weighed down by all those rocks.

Opportunity for Illumination

What rocks can you put down today?

Are you holding onto some rocks? Have you been paying attention to how heavy they make you feel? Try this: Collect a bag full of rocks from your local park, or go to a nearby craft store and buy a bag of river rocks. Put some of them in your pockets and walk around with them for a while, just to experience how heavy they make you feel. Next get a sharpie. On each rock, write the name of the person or reason for the rock. Then find a nearby body of water—a puddle, a pond, a lake, a stream, an ocean. One by one, toss your rocks into the water. Let them go.

Take a few deep breaths in, and with every exhale, offer a quiet thank you.

Was that easy or difficult? Why? Write about the experience in your journal.

The Spark

What Hurts

When my daughter was around three, she got a scratch on her finger the size of nothing at all, and the next morning she was complaining that it hurt so *bad* that she needed a Band-Aid immediately. As with every morning, I was rushing to get us all out the door and so I very distractedly said something completely dismissive to the effect of "You're fine; that doesn't hurt," probably without evening looking at her. Then I heard her say, in a very quiet but steady voice, "Mommy, how do you know what hurts if you're not me?"

How do you know what hurts if you're not me?

Um... Yow.

I took a breath, looked her in the eye, and said, "You're right, honey. Only you know how you feel. I'm so sorry," as she nodded at me with that wise look/sigh only young children master—that look that says, "Oh, you poor, poor adult who has forgotten once more all the rules and important things."

Of course while I was marveling at how obviously brave and brilliant and astute she was, I was also pretty certain that she really was just angling for attention and a princess Band-Aid.

But still. She could not be more right. I can never assume to know what hurts for someone else, just as I wouldn't want anyone to tell me what hurts for me.

It got me thinking about all the ways that I dismiss others' feelings—how often I get impatient if someone is upset by something that I don't think they should be upset by; how I brush off people's physical complaints if they seem overly exaggerated or dramatic; or how I try to gloss over people's hurt feelings so we can hurry and get to the sunny resolution. And that's just not really fair at all. Just because I don't see the hurt, that doesn't mean the hurt isn't there. It's not my job to determine the validity of the hurt; it's my job to simply be there. To say: "That must be so hard." To say: "I'm so sorry." To offer a hug. To offer a princess Band-Aid.

Opportunity for Illumination

How can you be there for what hurts today?

To what, or to whom, can you offer a princess Band-Aid, whether that is in the form of a phone call, a coffee, or simply a "how *are* you?"

The Spark

Lift Off

I hate the takeoff portion of flying. Since I am typically on an airplane once a month or more, you would think this is an issue that would have subsided by now, but alas.

For me, it's a few things: It's the shift from sitting completely still to getting the clearance for takeoff and beginning the awkward, lumbering acceleration down the runway. It's the deafening noise and the rattling of the entire plane. It's the feeling, when we first become airborne, of the wings tilting this way and that, as if the plane is trying to find balance in the air. It's how the heaviness of the plane itself seems to always be on the verge of sending us straight back to the ground—scoffing at the notion that such a beast could fly. I find my body literally clenching from the tension of these early moments, especially when I am flying in weather conditions that cause the airplane to dramatically swoop and jerk with the wind.

But then we always reach that magical cruising altitude. That sweet spot in the sky, where the plane does indeed find its balance. Where the noise softens, the plane steadies, and the pilot tells us to go about with our chosen electronics. Am I the only one who breathes a silent breath of relief and gratitude in that moment?

I was thinking how this is also the way it goes with new projects or ideas—or really, anything new. Starting is the hardest part. Starting can feel horrible. It can be messy and awkward and lumbering and scary. And in the early stages, it can be easy to believe that whatever it is we're trying to achieve is impossible—that there is *no way* it will lift off the ground. And then, even when it *does* lift off initially, it can suffer some turbulence along the way. It can tilt and sway awhile as it tries to find balance—whether that be in the form of support or funding or acceptance or excitement. But if we just hang in there, the magical cruising altitude is usually there somewhere. If we hang in there, we eventually realize that indeed, we can fly.

So, in the end we just need to trust the takeoff. Trust that despite the noise and the rattle and the labor the plane *will* lift off the ground. Trust that we will achieve flight and not worry when it feels like it's hard getting there. And when we see those around us struggling with the takeoff of something new, we can remind them too.

Opportunity for Illumination

What can you lift off today?

Is there a project you've been putting off starting? Is there a phone call you've been avoiding? Is there a hobby you've been circling but haven't taken the plunge? Is there a relationship you'd like to begin, or begin anew? Journal about it/them, and ask yourself these questions:

• What is the thing that needs to take off?

• What things will likely occur in the inevitable bumpy beginning? What will you encounter?

• What are the positive outcomes that await you if you can get through that initial takeoff?

• What are three steps you can take to move yourself closer to lifting off the ground?

The Spark

Waiting for the Scary Thing

As I approached the due date of my first child, I remember telling people that I felt like I was in a haunted house. When you're in a haunted house, you know you're going to be scared, you just don't know *when*, so you walk around with your shoulders tense and your eyes half shut until the zombie finally jumps out at you and relieves you of the tension of waiting for it to happen. Same thing with the baby. I knew this baby was coming. I just didn't know when, so I was walking around in constant trepidation—is this the moment? Is it now? Fear can do that to us, no matter what the thing is we are fearing.

For example, one year spring came early in Indiana; seriously, summer had practically arrived by March. And with the joys of spring come some nuisances too; specifically, that spring brought wasps. We had spotted a few flying around the perimeter of the house and even in our garage, but then one morning one flew right over the heads of my daughter and me while I was brushing her hair in her bathroom. A wasp in our house! Now, I'm a self-admitted scaredy cat when it comes to insects, especially ones with the means to inflict bodily harm. So after that I started walking around my house with my shoulders tense, looking up at the ceilings and in the crevices with dreaded anticipation of the next wasp. Is this the moment? Is it now?

Another example. Years ago, my brother got stung by a scorpion that was nestled in his shoe. For a long time after that I would shake out my shoes before putting them on despite the fact that I've never lived in any place that would also be inhabited by scorpions.

That same brother suffered a brain aneurysm a few years ago, followed subsequently by a stroke. He survived both, and made a full and miraculous recovery. Early in his recovery, we all kept trying to help him with things, support him in his walking, and just generally protect him from any further ill. But during that time, he smartly kept us at arm's length, saying, "You know, I'm *going* to fall."

It reminds me of a story by my favorite artist/storyteller Brian Andreas, Storypeople, which goes like this. "Leaning out as far as she can, hoping she'll fall soon, so she can stop worrying about whether it will happen or not."

Because, the thing is, The Scary Thing will happen. The baby will be born. The zombie will jump out at you. The wasp (or scorpion) will sting you. You will fall. Waiting for these things, anticipating them, just adds to your agony, and worse, makes you miss out on just enjoying the journey of life. There's a difference between being careful (*I totally got some pest control for those wasps, and I admit I still sometimes shake out my shoes*) and being immobilized.

Opportunity for Illumination

Are you letting fear of The Scary Thing hold you back?

What's your scary thing? How you can say "I'm Not Afraid Of YOU!" to the Scary Thing, and begin to move past it?

The Spark

Ghost Story

What's real and what's fiction?

I love this question, asked to a group of us once by a very clever coworker and storyteller.

Here's one for you.

Between my freshman and sophomore years of college, I was back home working for the summer. We lived in a farmhouse that was over one hundred years old. One morning, home alone before work, I stood leaning against the kitchen sink, staring out of the window. Our dog, Zack, was enjoying a morning snooze on the landing at the bottom of the stairs. The house was completely quiet. I remember the moment so vividly, even more than twenty years later, mostly for its absolute nothingness.

Suddenly, I heard Zack growl. I looked over and saw him standing at the bottom of the stairs, staring wide eyed up to the top. He was standing rigid, the fur on his neck up on end. I couldn't see what was at the top of the stairs because there was a wall covering the stairwell; whatever it was scared the heck out of him, and he couldn't take his eyes off it. He growled again, barked once, and hightailed it out of there, running past me and out of the screen door. I figured I could go investigate what exactly was at the top of the stairs, or I could trust his sound doggy-advice and get a move on. I chose option B, hightailing it out of there right on his heels toward my car, which happened to be parked directly in front of the window that looked out from the top of the stairs. As I walked toward my car, I felt the hairs stand up on the back of my head. I felt *watched* from that window and not in any kind of friendly "Oh, hi, how's it going?" sort of way.

What's real, what's fiction?

That story I told you is real. It *really* happened. But what happened, exactly? My dog growled, and I got spooked. Is it fiction to say that I had myself a ghost encounter back at that farmhouse? Maybe. But all these years I've told it as my ghost story. That's the way I remember it, the way I experienced it.

There are very few absolute truths out there. Maybe gravity. And $E = MC^2$. And the Law of Whenever The Power Goes Out All I Can Think Of To Do Is Things That Require Electricity. But my point is this: what's *real* to me is a composite of my experiences, my beliefs, my feelings. What's real to you is your composite. They might be similar, but most likely, they will be different.

I think sometimes people equate the "truth" with the "facts." But the problem with that is that facts are just the quantifiable things that happen. *Stories* are what we do with those facts, and our lives are woven by our stories.

What's real and what's fiction? Life is not black and white. It is solidly gray. So, when you are tempted to judge or dismiss another person's "truth," think of your own "ghost story" and handle that person with care.

Opportunity for Illumination

How can you honor what's "real"?

Write down some of your favorite stories from your childhood, adolescence, or adulthood. The stories you love to tell, or that others love to tell about you. Next, invite a friend to coffee and encourage him/her to bring a few stories of their own. Share your stories with each other. Jot down any reflections about the experience.

The Spark

On Illuminating

Ah, to illuminate. It has been defined as: *to supply or brighten with light; to make lucid or clear; to throw light on; to enlighten, or—* my favorite—*to make resplendent or illustrious.* Resplendent or Illustrious! How great is that?

When things are illuminated, it is as if they have a light shining upon them. When you are illuminated, *you* are a light.

But, Jeez Louise it can be *hard* to do. G. K. Chesterton said, "It's easy to be heavy; hard to be light." Just like sometimes the ease of staying curled up can be more tempting than the vulnerability of unfolding, sometimes the dark feels just fine, thank you very much. To illuminate means, in some ways, to have a spotlight on yourself. When we are illuminated, and when we seek to provide illumination for others, we are exposed. We are out there, saying Hello, WORLD! This is ME!!!

But I think to live illuminated and to be open to receive the illumination shining from others, is one of the most *alive* ways we can live. It allows us the greatest opportunity to connect with our family, our friends, our community, our jobs, our hobbies, our passions, our fears, our talents. Illumination, in some ways, gives you the permission to be wholly and unapologetically you.

So go be resplendent. Be illustrious. The day awaits.

Opportunity for Illumination

How are you a light to others?

Think of the three people you interviewed at the start of this chapter. How were/are they a light to you? Now, think of how you are a light to others. Whom do you think you are a light for, and how?

Chapter Four: Ignite

Overview

Okay! You've awakened, you've unfolded, you've illuminated. And now it's time to IGNITE! Time to throw back the fears and the what ifs and the maybes and the dreads and the doubts, and declare it GAME ON. Ignition, to me, is about action. It is extreme awareness and presence.

Before we dive in, create a mini "vision board" that represents the Ultimate You. The You that makes you say "heck, yeah!" The You that is living life to the fullest. If you have any pictures of yourself where you were captured in a moment of extreme courage or where you were feeling particularly beautiful or where you felt fearless, be sure to include them. Otherwise feel free to use magazine cutouts, crayons or markers, or any other artistic means to create this visual of the Ultimate You. It can be as small as an index card or as big as a poster board. This isn't the time for judgment or editing—instead it's time for everything the Ultimate You can be and could be (and of course, already is). Have fun and don't hold back! There are no rules here.

Once you've finished your board, put it somewhere where you might see it daily. Then, go sit somewhere—a quiet park bench, a coffee shop, a porch swing—somewhere where you can just sit and stare quietly for at least ten minutes. Just sit, and let your mind wander. At the end of the ten minutes, jot down any observations in your journal.

The Spark

Awareness

One day I was leaving a store equipped with automated doors—the kind that open as you walk toward them, leaving you with no greater job but to keep walking. I was literally millimeters away from smashing my face into the glass, when it occurred to me that the automatic doors were not, in fact, working. I put my hand out just in time to open the door that had betrayed me, shaking my head at my complete and total lack of awareness.

This reminded me of the time, more than twenty years ago, that I went skydiving. It was a "static line" skydive, which has you tethered in such a way that your parachute automatically opens. This way, you don't have to worry about remembering to open it before plummeting to the earth.

Additionally, our helmets were equipped with radios so the nice men on the ground could give us instructions on how to steer ourselves to a safe and gentle landing. Now, before actually going up in the plane, we spent some number of hours training for all the "what if" scenarios, including how to land ourselves safely and gently to the ground without their guidance, in the unlikely event that our helmet radios malfunctioned.

After the training, we went up in the plane. I tell you, I have never known fear like the fear I felt when that plane door opened and it was my time to climb out of the plane and onto the wing. I mean, seriously. How was I not just going to get sucked out into the ether?

But, my parachute opened as expected (thank you, universe). My helmet radio was working (thanks again, universe). It was a gorgeous, sunny day (oh universe, you're so good to me). So, I settled in to enjoy the slow journey back to earth. I breathed deep. I listened to a beautiful silence that I imagine can only be accomplished at such heights. I felt the warm breeze and soaked in the sun.

And then it occurred to me that the earth was not so far away anymore. And then it further occurred to me that I hadn't heard the nice men on the ground talk in my helmet for a while. I started to watch a particular cornfield get closer and closer and I thought, "Wow, that cornfield sure is getting close," and then I heard the nice men in my helmet say, "Prepare for a crash landing!" as I tumbled head over foot straight into said cornfield. Nice.

So, what happened? Those nice men on the ground "lost me in the sun," and by the time they found me again, it was too late to guide me safely and gently to the ground. All the while, of course, I had all the tools to land myself—I mean, they spent the whole day training us for just such a scenario—I just didn't use them. I expected them to do it for me.

Total. Lack. Of. Awareness.

Just like that day with the automatic door. I do believe I know the proper procedures for opening a door; I just didn't use them when I expected the door to open for me.

How often does this happen? A door smashing our face or a tumble into a cornfield might highlight such moments, but how

often do we take a passive approach to our lives, expecting a thing
to just *happen* for us? Expecting others to do it for us? Expecting
everything we need to just be there? I feel like I'm an active
participant in my life, but moments like these make me reconsider.
What other door am I about to smash into because I'm simply not
paying attention? Because, while there are certainly many things
in life that we just can't influence, there are many others that we
can—especially if we make a conscious choice to open our own
door or steer our own parachute.

Opportunity for Ignition

How can you be a fully active participant in your life?

Take a moment to "look around" your life. What are you not paying attention to? What are you waiting for someone to do for you? What doors might be about ready to smash you in the face? What cornfield might be looming? Write about it in your journal.

The Spark

Game On

While we all have moments of unawareness in our lives—those things that totally take us by surprise when they hit—we also have things that we are aware of, but just avoiding. Do you know what I mean?

When my daughter was around five, she once started singing "Let's Call The Whole Thing Off." You know, potayto, potahto, only she revised it spectacularly to go "Let's call the whole thing ON!"

When I first heard her adaptation, I chuckled to myself. And then I had a gut-wrenching realization. How often do I just "call the whole thing off" when faced with a disagreement or misunderstanding? How often do I say or think to myself "oh, just forget it?" when something isn't going smoothly? How often do I stop when something starts to feel hard? The truth? A lot.

In an extreme attempt to avoid conflict AT ALL COSTS, I can easily default to trying to let things smooth over, or of brushing them under the rug, or looking the other way. I don't ruffle feathers. I don't "lean in." Heck, I've been known to lean so far out I practically fall out the window. Sure, this strategy can be effective in a lot of situations—I believe that there is extreme value to rolling with the punches and going with the flow. I am proud of my "not easily offended-ness." But do I perhaps sometimes use that to hide from the hard things? Um.

So what if I started trying to "call the whole thing ON" instead? What if I said "I'm sorry" if I feel like I said or did the wrong thing, no matter how small? What if I said "I don't agree with you" if someone says something that I don't agree with? What if I said "Hey, that hurt my feelings!" or "Could you explain that?" Would the world end? I doubt it. Would I get embarrassed and blush and feel awkward and possibly even cry? Probably. Would it be worth it? I have a sneaking suspicion that most of the time the answer is yes.

Also, and most importantly: what made my daughter singing the song all the more delightful was that the declaration of "calling the whole thing ON" came with a sense of excitement and joy, not dread. It was as if she was saying: "We disagree? Yippee! Game ON—let's work this out!" I love this, because it means that instead of running away from the problem, suddenly there *is* no problem, there is only an opportunity.

I think that maybe the more I practice "calling the whole thing ON," the better I'll get, the less awkward I'll feel, and the more I'll realize that I'm actually *leaning in* to what matters—greater connections, deeper relationships and probably even better sleep at night. And to that I say, Game ON! What about you?

Opportunity for Ignition

Something you've been avoiding? How can you "call the whole thing ON" today?

Make a list in your journal of some things you've been avoiding—a difficult conversation, a glimpse at your credit card statement, a request for a raise, a bold new haircut—whatever it is, write it down without judgment. Next, think of one step you could take today to declare it GAME ON for at least one of those things. Even if it's a baby step. Once you've taken a step, reflect about what happened and how it felt.

The Spark

Within The Lines

I am the world's worst parker.

Even if I was the sole car in a cavernous parking lot, I would still park crooked, or too close to the lines. I simply can't park straight and centered within the lines of a parking spot. Can't do it.

I believe this is a reflection of my genius.

Clearly, I cannot be confined by lines. I think I must still intuitively know what very young children know—lines are meant to be "suggestions," mere guides on what choices you *might* make with your crayon or your minivan.

As children we learn to color within the lines. We work very hard to do this. I remember when my daughter was young and became so dogged in her determination to color within the lines that she held my husband hostage for nearly an hour at an arts and crafts table. This is a good thing; it helps the development of fine motor skills, it helps us learn how to draw specific shapes and figures. Many have argued that an artist *needs* a canvas on which to paint—a natural boundary. Within the limits of the canvas an artist can be free to create; the "lines" create freedom.

All this said, I think sometimes we take the whole "stay within the lines" concept a bit too far, and in doing so, squelch our children's natural instincts to explore, discover, create.

As adults we are obsessed with "staying within the lines" too, but not just in coloring books (though watch any parent coloring next to their child and you will see some pretty meticulous don't-interrupt-my-staying-within-the-lines-crayon-work). No, our lines are different. They are lines that establish how we should dress, how we should act, what kind of job we should seek, what kind of dwelling we should establish, what our opinions are.

Lines are important. There is value to them and there is a time and a place for them. But they aren't the only options. We can make our own lines, and those can be valuable too.

Also, when you make your own lines, don't worry too much about how perfectly you stay within them—sometimes a little bit crooked is a lot beautiful.

Opportunity for Ignition

How can you redesign the lines?

In your journal, draw a map that shows your typical route to school/work/errands on any given day.

Now draw a NEW map that shows an alternative route that you can try. Then, actually go try that new route!

Once you've tried your new route, jot any thoughts about it. Did you notice anything new? Was it faster/slower/better/more uncomfortable/surprising/annoying?

Based on your experiences remapping your actual route, are there any other "maps" that you can reroute in your life? Any other lines you can draw anew?

The Spark

Going Once

When my children were both in preschool, the school held an annual Spring Fling: a weekend filled with face painting and games and treats, along with a silent auction of all sorts of goodies and baskets up for the bidding, with the proceeds going to a few wonderful charities. One year my daughter locked in on the basket of her dreams—a splash of pink and black and sparkles, so I put a bid in. When our name wasn't called, she was devastated. Truly, she wept the entire car ride home. She just couldn't understand why we didn't get the basket, and it took her weeks to get over it.

The next year, I was determined not to let that happen again. We strolled through the aisles, and I asked her to name a few different baskets she liked. She picked a few, and then of course found THE ONE that she wanted above all else—a little "rock star" basket with a toy guitar and microphone. I figured I would bid on several things, hoping that we might get lucky with one. The whole time, I was overemphasizing the uncertainty of it all, reminding her that just because we bid on something doesn't mean we get it, telling her in fact that we most likely wouldn't get anything, and that was okay. (Especially since my version of bidding is akin to an amateur poker player—a penny here, a dollar there.) She seemed to understand, but I was still half-tempted to skip out before the winning numbers were even called.

But we stayed, and when it came time for the winners to be announced, a sheet was placed outside the auction room with all the winning numbers. And lo—our number was there! I happily told my daughter that we had won something, and she practically jumped out of her pants in excitement. We ran into the room and waited in line to find out which of the baskets would be our lucky one. When we got up to the front, the scene went something like this:

School: Erika, what was your number?

Me: Sixty-four.

School: Oh, yes! Sixty-four! You won three baskets!

Me: (blink, blink)... Three?

Daughter: *THREE?!?!??!* (fainting with the joy of it all—truly, it was as if she had just won the $400 million jackpot. I thought she was going to burst out of her skin.)

Watching my daughter literally skip down the hallway of the school, clutching two of her new treasured baskets tightly to her chest (including the rock star basket), declaring proudly to everyone she walked past "I won three baskets! I won three baskets!" I marveled at how different the scene was from just the year before.

Apparently, this auction thing can go both ways. You can walk away empty handed, or you can walk away with much, much more than you budgeted, I mean bargained, for.

Somehow this feels kind of like life. You win some, and you lose some. It can be tempting to just skip it altogether—to avoid the pain of losing, we simply don't jump in. We skip the auction. But to that I say, if you don't risk the horrible pain of walking away empty handed, you will never know the exquisite joy of having your arms overflowing with more than you ever wished for.

Opportunity for Ignition

How can you get in the auction today?

Where have you experienced disappointment, whether recently or not? Write down any ways you might try to "get back in the auction." Is there a way you can try again? Ask again? Reach out again?

Then, when you're *ready*, go do the thing(s) you've written. And depending on the result, feel free to add a "Sold!" or a "Nice Try!" note next to the disappointment listed. Because sometimes things will work out, and sometimes they won't. But you never know until you try.

The Spark

Help

Just before my son turned two, he decided to take very seriously the phase commonly known as the "terrible twos." He discovered a desire for independence and had already started to find the vocabulary to vocalize it. Some of his favorite phrases were: "I do it!" and "I turn!" and "I hold it!" and "No, stop!" He also found the three-letter word most beloved by children across the ages: WHY. For him, it would come out like "WuuEEYYEE?!?!" after each time he was told no. No, you can't climb on that table. No, you can't go near the fireplace. No, you can't pour all the cereal on the floor.

One of the things he became very clear about in that time was that he'd much prefer to do it himself, thank you very much, no matter what "it" was. This was where the "I do it!" replayed itself over and over throughout the day. When asked if he needed help, he was also known to reply "/ help!" He just wanted to figure things out on his own, without help or guidance, even when the task was totally beyond his scope or ability.

It was fascinating to watch and interesting to think about how often we do this even as adults. That stubborn determination to "do it" without help can be a great way to learn new skills and stretch ourselves to new heights, but it can also block us from receiving much needed guidance and perspective. Sometimes "help" is the best thing that could happen to us—it's just really,

really hard to ask for.

I remember a story from one of my colleagues where she was at a family function and, as happens, the kids were all playing in one part of the house and the adults were mingling in and around the kitchen. The adults noticed one of the kids run into the kitchen, turn on the sink faucet, scoop as much water into his hands as would fit, and then run back to where the other kids were. They watched him repeat this several times before someone finally asked what he was doing. His response, simply, was "The fire is almost out!"

The fire is almost out.

I know that, for me, asking for help can feel vulnerable. It can feel like a sign of failure, perhaps admittance that I can't do it all or that I can't do it well, and that can be all too humbling. I'd like to believe that I can conquer any fire. However, when I think about the other side of the equation—when *I'm* asked to help someone—far from judging what I know that person perceives to be their weakness or failure, I am simply grateful for the opportunity to lend them my love and support.

Now. I just need to remember that when it's my turn to ask.

Like the quote goes, "The spaces between your fingers were created so that another's could fill them in" (unknown).

Opportunity for Ignition

Where can you ask for help?

What do you need help with? And whom can you ask? And why *haven't* you asked? Journal about that. And then go ask them. If not all of them, *some* of them. Write your observations about what happens.

The Spark

Monster Mom

I have days where I become a Monster Mom. Days when my children have taken my patience to the limits and then sent it flying off a cliff, and as a response I hear myself being snarky, snappy, and sarcastic. Do you know about days like these? Seriously, I wouldn't be anywhere close to that big of a jerk with anyone else on earth—even people who might deserve a little snappiness from me—and yet there I am, failing the two people I love most wholly and deeply on this entire planet.

At the end of my Monster Mom days, I just want to curl under the covers and cry—so sad for not having more patience, for not being more loving, for letting myself get so upset at them, and for what? Really, just being kids, in the end. They are learning and finding their way in this world. Why can't I give them space to do that already? Why do I expect them to act like fully formed and rational adults? And also, how is it possible for me to go from Super Mom to Monster Mom to Meh Mom and right back to Super Mom again all within the same hour, much less the same day? Even if you are not a parent, do you have Monster Boss moments? Monster Friend? Monster Waiter-In-Line-Person? Moments where you become a monster, perhaps moments after you were acting super?

The problem with those Monster moments of course—other than the certainty that my actions will cause my children to close their hearts to the world and pay thousands of dollars in future therapy—is that thinking of my Monster Mom behavior makes me think about all the other ways I am, and have ever been, a jerk. I let down my team at work because of dropped communication; I was rude to the waitress who wouldn't allow substitutions on the menu; I forgot to send my friend a birthday card; I didn't eat right or exercise *again* today; and man, how is anyone who knew me in my ever-so-annoying college days even still friends with me, seriously?

The list could go on and on, and it's a dark and stormy list. It's both trivial and too deep to comprehend. And it's inviting me to stay and wallow.

But if I stay and wallow, then I'm not trying again. I'm not trying again to be loving and joyous and forgiving with my children. I'm not trying again to be nicer to the idiotic... I mean nice... waitress. I'm not trying again to let someone know that I'm thinking about them.

We all talk a lot about forgiveness and forgiving ourselves, and it occurs to me now that sometimes it is even much simpler and more difficult than that. Don't wait to forgive yourself—carry on beating yourself up if you'd like. Just show up and keep trying again and again while you're at it. Because those at the receiving end don't know what we're thinking, they just know what we've *done*. I think my children don't pay as much attention to my Monster Mom moments as I do, especially when I follow them up with Super Mom moments. I think my friend appreciates a belated birthday card or even a simple text message, as much as a perfectly packaged and on-time one. Simply, I think most of us are much less Monster-ish and much more Super-ish than we might think we are, especially when we just keep trying.

So I may pour myself a glass of wine and sulk about the fact that I snapped at my precious children, but while I'm doing that I'm also going to take a deep breath, get down on the floor, and play "school" for the five thousandth time today and I'm going to be the best dang student they've ever seen (until the moment maybe I'm not).

Opportunity for Ignition

Have you had any "monster" moments lately?

Moments where you don't show up with your best self? If so, how can you keep showing up and just try again?

The Spark

On Igniting

To me, *Wings & Whimsy* is about living fully, all while living very imperfectly. Showing up, owning up, and embracing all there is to you—and trying to do the same for others. Because life is too short to sell ourselves short, and life is too short to sell our experiences short, and life is too short to sell others short. Life is too short.

I love the word "ignite." It's one of my favorite words, because it's so... *sparkly*. And since it literally means "to set on fire," I love the idea of it setting our hearts on fire, our souls on fire, our passions on fire. To ignite something is to bring it to life or perhaps bring it *back* to life. It's also a spark. It's the on button. It's about being fully in *it*, whatever it is.

We all have the opportunity to both be ignited and to ignite. When I think about moments in my life where I've been ignited, it spans the spectrum from something I've seen on the news to an idea that just won't let go to a person I've connected with. The things that ignite me are different, but what they all have in common is that they light a fire in me that won't be ignored. They take me from the "maybe someday I'll... " place to the "I have got to do something NOW" place. It's the pivotal moment, the proverbial moment of truth. And when I think of times where I've been the igniter, it's usually about helping someone set something in motion—an idea, a belief, a dream, a plan.

As I said at the beginning, to me ignition is action. It takes all the *thoughts* inherent in awakening and unfolding and illuminating and turns them into actions. And our actions create our lives.

There is magic in ignition, because it also implies a start. First a spark, and then a flame. And a start is a promise. A start is ripe with possibilities. Ignition, it turns out, gets us right back to commencing.

And the circle begins again. Do you see what I mean? We're constantly rotating through different levels of awareness and illumination and ignition in different areas of our lives and with different people in our lives.

Opportunity for Ignition

What can you ignite today?

If you're like me, the person who gets the least amount of ignition from you is *you*. But we know this isn't okay, because how can we ignite others if we're not ignited ourselves?

Look back at the Vision Board of the "Ultimate You" you created at the start of this chapter. First, and most importantly, think about days where you might have some of those "monster" moments. It's okay if you're not living up to your Ultimate You every day—of course you won't. What's most important is that you just keep showing up, that you just keep trying.

But to ignite yourself, to give energy toward that Ultimate You, what step(s) can you take today that would bring you closer to that image? Whether it's buying Wonder Woman underwear, signing up for a class, calling a friend, building a house, running for office, or finally leaving, write your ideas in your journal.

(And then get to it.)

Chapter Five: Howl

Overview

In *awakening* you allowed your eyes to open around a certain topic or topics. In *unfolding* you peeled back some layers and maybe discovered some things that were wow-worthy in your life. In *illuminating* you brought light on things that may have previously been in the dark—looking at who was illuminating to you and how you are illuminating to others. And in *igniting* you allowed yourself to catch fire, turning thought into action. In this chapter, "Howl," you will once again celebrate the beauty of YOU, but perhaps with more courage this time, as we end where we begin (always).

Before we dive in, take another read of the commencement speech I wrote in the prelude of the book. Then, take a quiet walk, or spend time sitting quietly on the couch, or take an extralong shower. Give yourself time to think about the things you've been exploring in this book. Then ask yourself, "What is most important to me?" Using the thoughts that emerge from that, start to write notes about what your own commencement speech would be. If the world is listening, what do you have to say?

The Spark

Dance Your Way Through

When I was in college, my family was vacationing in Florida and we went to one of those Human Mazes. My mom, stepdad, sister, and I all went in together. My mom quickly maneuvered her way through the maze and settled in at the viewing platform where successful maze-goers could look upon their hapless companions still wandering the cavernous field. Meanwhile, back in the maze, my stepdad found the nearest emergency exit and my sister crawled under the hedges to get out. I, however, went round and round in circles trying to complete the maze, frustration growing with every wrong turn. In the blazing Florida sun, I was blinded by sweat and irritation, dismayed at my inability to solve the puzzle.

Suddenly I heard my mom yell from the victors' platform: "Just dance your way through it!" I remember thinking, "Just dance my way through it? What does that even mean?" Of course I was annoyed with her for being all advice and confidence, she from the victor's platform. And then I was defensive—I know how to get out of a maze! And finally I decided it might be smart to listen to her, given that she was, in fact, free, while I was the one still trapped inside.

So I closed my eyes, took a deep breath, and relaxed. I thought for a moment about dancing and how when you're dancing for pure pleasure you're not really thinking about anything; you're just enjoying the sounds, the feeling, the joy of the moment. I opened my eyes and decided to stop thinking about how to get out of the maze; rather, I just followed the sounds around me and let my body follow the feeling of the maze. And you know what? I was out within minutes.

Since that day, I've thought a lot about what it means to "dance my way through," and I realize that in most situations, when I think too much, worry too much, try too hard, or allow frustration to take over, I falter. But when I am able to relax in the present moment, enjoy all that surrounds me, and breathe in the air, I thrive. The advice to "dance my way through" has also reminded me to take life more lightly. This was probably one of the first moments that I became keenly aware that the most profound lessons often come out of the most ordinary situations—that the extraordinary hides within the ordinary.

Opportunity for Howling

"Dance Your Way Through" has become my life mantra. What's Yours?

Come up with a phrase that will remind you to HOWL when faced with those moments in life that make you falter. Then, is there a picture, symbol, or image that might represent that phrase? Draw that next to the phrase.

The Spark

That Is Ridiculous!

So what stops us from howling? I think I know. I think we all know, deep inside.

Fear.

Such a small word to describe an often all-consuming emotion.

I once was in a staff meeting where a clever and creative colleague of mine led us in an activity about fears based on a spell from the *Harry Potter* book series that allows you to turn something you fear into something to laugh at by transforming the thing you fear into something ridiculous.

And I remember thinking: That. Is. Brilliant.

In talking about our deepest fears with my colleagues, someone brought up their fear of airplanes. Ironically, I was flying later that night, so it was on my mind as I was sitting at the airport bar waiting for my flight, sipping a glass of "confidence wine." As I sat there, a father and daughter walked up. The daughter said, "What are we doing?" and the dad replied, "I'm just getting something before we get on this silly flight," (a shot of "confidence Jameson").

I don't typically describe myself as someone who is afraid to fly, but every time my plane hits the runway, I call upon my guardian angels, a legion of fairies, the gods, the control tower, and anyone else who might be listening, to protect the flight and carry us safely home.

Why are we afraid to fly? I would imagine for the same reason we are afraid of most things—the perceived or real lack of control we feel when facing them.

Control of any sort really is nothing but an illusion, and when it comes to things we're afraid of, that feeling of helplessness can be overpowering. That is why I think having the courage to declare something ridiculous is so powerful—it allows us to claim power where once we've felt none. It forces us to laugh in the face of those things that are holding us back, limiting us, and blocking our way.

Now. There is also a difference between laughing in the face of fears that are perhaps unfounded (like my fear of sharks from land-locked Indiana) or that are magnified (like the fear of that upcoming presentation) and defying very real life-threatening scenarios. So, to be clear: I should most definitely tell myself "That is *ridiculous*" about my fear of sharks, especially when I am not currently in the water. But one should NOT call a massive approaching hurricane "ridiculous" when one lives near water at sea level. Similarly, if I ever did have the unfortunate occasion to find myself face-to-face with a Great White, laughing and pointing and shouting "HaHaHaHa! You're ridiculous!" would definitely *not* be my most effective choice. No, the ability to declare something ridiculous is not for all occasions, but when it is fitting, its power is... well, magical.

Opportunity for Howling

So today, as you contemplate the things that you are afraid of, overwhelmed by, avoiding, feeling Very Uncomfortable about: What can you declare to be ridiculous?

Think of something you've either wanted to do or something you've wanted to believe about yourself. Something that nags at you in the quiet of the night or in the face that stares back at you from the mirror. Maybe it's in the form of a wish: *I wish I could write; I wish I had the courage to go back to school; I wish I could sing in front of a crowd. Or maybe it's in the form of an inner critic: I'm not smart enough; I don't listen to my kids; I'll never get that promotion; I'm just not funny.*

First, make a "dump" list of all those things.

Then, pick one to turn around, to declare ridiculous. So, if my first thought was "No one cares to hear my stories," my turn around would be "My stories are worth telling."

Write your turnaround sentence in your journal.

Finally, take a whole pack of Post-its and write your turnaround sentence on as many of them as you can muster, and post them all around—on your mirror, on your dashboard, on your computer monitor, in your sock drawer, by the coffee machine. Keep them up for one day or one month, but allow yourself to read that sentence over and over. During this time, write any thoughts or reflections about this activity.

The Spark

Leave the Edges Wild

A friend once forwarded me an episode of the series *The Song That Changed My Life*, which focused on a Cincinnati-based band called Over the Rhine. While I don't listen to their music, I found myself drawn in. The episode highlighted the life of the husband and wife team who make up the band, as well as the farmhouse and expansive land that make up their home. In it, the husband references something his father said many years back. He remembers that when they moved onto the land (which they named Nowhere Farm), his father told him to "leave the edges of this place wild. Let the songbirds have their wild hidden places."

Like the musician in its recounting of it, I was absolutely struck by the power in that advice: *leave the edges of this place wild.*

Sometimes, I do the opposite: I try to plan and control and account for every aspect of a thing, whatever that thing is. Be it a meeting, a party, a visit, an event, a conversation, I feel like I should have it all figured out from start to finish, not wanting to leave anything untended. I think there is *some* value to that—I mean, guests to this house will never go hungry or thirsty or lacking in treats. But it can also add a layer of stress that isn't necessary and can unintentionally constrict the possibilities that are only found in those wild edges.

It occurs to me that the universe understands the wisdom in this too, and will remind us of it by throwing a monkey wrench in our best laid plans. A child gets sick on the day of an important meeting with a client; an outdoor party gets rained out; time runs out; communication fails. We can easily look at these things as annoyances; they could have ruined our day or caused a hassle. But I think they might just be opportunities to let go of our need for control, to allow life to go the way it's *going* to go—not necessarily the way we *think* it should go.

Storyteller Brian Andreas, Storypeople, has this to say about it: "If you hold onto the handle, she said, it's easier to maintain the illusion of control. But it's more fun if you just let the wind carry you."

I know that during weeks, when I find a lot weighing heavily on my mind, at least a part of it is because I'm trying to clear away all the wild spaces. I'm clawing for answers, for perfection, for a glossy finish. But I think sometimes it's better to just head toward the wild edges and listen to what the songbirds have to say.

Opportunity for Howling

How can you leave the edges wild?

What have you been trying to clean up? What have you been trying to fix? What leaves you restless because it's not "good enough"? Is there an opportunity to leave any of those things "wild"?

The Spark

Sometimes It's Really That Simple

When I was about seventeen, some friends and I went to a big arena concert of the band Whitesnake. Due to a lack of finances *and* a lack of planning, our seats were literally the very last row of the very top of the farthest section possible away from the stage. But, hey, it was the '80s, and Whitesnake was KING, and we just wanted to be there for it.

And then this happened:

A local radio station had been promoting that they would be giving away all sorts of freebies, including presumably very good seats, on the night of the concert. As we walked into the arena, I casually grabbed two bumper stickers from the station's advertisement table, not quite sure what I would do with them or how on earth we would be noticed in our next-zip-code-over seats.

The radio station had staff members walking around inside holding the power of God to simply point at the random people they felt had earned a prize or an upgrade. Winding our way through the hordes of people, we marveled at the lengths some people had gone to in order to get those upgrades. Full radio station paraphernalia from head to toe, outlandish costumes, signs, scantily clad groupies, you name it.

When I spotted one of the radio station staffers heading toward our section, I did the only thing I could think to do: I quickly slapped the two bumper stickers on the back pockets of my jeans, turned around, danced and shouted a bit, then turned back around to discover him pointing my way and gesturing for me to come down with a friend. Stunned, I grabbed one of my equally stunned buddies, and we ran toward this Glorious Giver of Good Things. He led us to our new seats: Front row. Center stage. It was unbelievable. We were immersed in the smoldering stares of David Coverdale, the screaming fans, the sweat, the electric guitars pulsating through the crowd. Steve Vai, a legendary guitarist, was touring with them at the time, and I even caught a guitar pick that he tossed into the crowd. This kind of thing does not happen when you are in Row ZZZZZ in Section 5,457.

I couldn't get over it. So many people had spent hours concocting ways to get the attention of the radio station, and my two last minute bumper stickers and a quick shake of my tush transformed my entire experience of that concert.

Now, I am definitely NOT promoting the idea that young men or women should use their bodies as advertisement, and I don't necessarily agree with my own teenager decision making. BUT. I do understand now that two very important realizations came out of that moment for me; first, an understanding that sometimes, things are really much simpler than we imagine them to be. And second, it is always a good idea to just go for it, even if you feel like you don't possibly have a chance. Who knew Whitesnake had so much to teach me, beyond the power of a good hair gel and a pair of leather pants?

The first realization is always on my mind each year when we approach holidays or special occasions—it's so easy to get caught up in the thoughts of what I *must* do to create a spectacular and transformative house, meal, decoration, present, experience. It's tempting to believe that more equals better. But sometimes more just equals *more*. But of course this plays out in many ways, not just at teenage rock concerts and holiday seasons. How often do we craft a lengthy explanation when really, a simple "I'm sorry; here's how I'm going to fix it" is better? How often do we fret about the state of our house when really, the unexpected visitor only cares about a cup of coffee and a listening ear? How often do we create elaborate systems and structures at work when really, just talking is better? Sometimes, it really is that simple.

So don't wait for "Is This Love" blaring out from your local radio station's "all '80s weekend" to remind you of this very important fact I learned all those years ago.

Opportunity for Howling

Are you making something more complicated than it needs to be? How can you simplify?

Inspired by my rock station bumper stickers from the '80s, go buy a pack of stickers to use in moments when you just need to stop thinking and *go for it.* Make them stickers that make you smile or laugh, stickers that bring out your inner child. Keep them somewhere handy—your purse, your wallet, your desk, your car. When you need that push, that burst of courage, that call to action, just grab a sticker put it on, and see what happens!

Write any reflections about what happens—or better yet, take a picture of yourself in your stickers and tape it in your journal!

The Spark

Grown Up

I swear sometimes I am STUNNED I am not still eighteen. When the weather is nice and the sun is shining, and when I am driving with the windows down, and when an '80s song comes on, well then I just KNOW that I am a carefree, young wisp of a girl driving her big old car and strumming to the beat. So imagine my shock when I hear strange sounds coming from behind me and turn to notice two small children demanding things like snacks and "better" music and look around to realize that I am actually a forty-something in a minivan. ... like, "wow—how on earth did I get *here*?!"

Yes, while the teenager lives strong in my mind, there is ample evidence to prove that's the only place she still lives: I catch my reflection in the side mirror and think "Who the heck is *that* old lady?" I interact with teenagers and they call me "ma'am" and "lady." My body groans and creaks when I get out of bed in the morning. I'm practical. And I can probably name only a third of the artists currently topping the charts. (But I can spot a Def Leppard song from a mile away.)

The funny thing about aging, to me anyway, is that because I still *feel* young, and probably because I am short and usually wearing jeans, most of the time I just feel like I'm *playing* grown up. You see, you all got the manual on being an adult; I must have moved that day. Some days it seems to me like the entire rest of the grown-up world has it together. You're all so smart! You're so organized! You're so official! You have nice furniture and investments and lawn services and you know where to shop for the best deals on avocados. You know the best back roads to avoid construction and you know what that rash on your child's neck means. You can whip together a healthy dinner in twenty minutes and you can fix the broken DVD player. You know how to clean up grease stains and you keep up with the laundry. You have accountants and all your documents are up to date. You use your smartphones as calendars and task planners. I can't even turn on the DVD player and I make the same meals every week and I always pay too much for avocados. I pick the wrong lane in traffic and in grocery stores. I have messy piles instead of organized files. My paper calendar is filled with scribbles and to-do lists (in multicolored pens, no less).

But, what does it mean to be a grown-up, after all? Is there a right way to do this thing? Once I stop comparing my version of being a grown-up to your version, I can actually embrace my inner teenager and all she still encourages me to do. Like dancing, even if the music is not from the '80s. Or laughing at really, really silly things. Or singing at the top of my lungs, really badly. Or appreciating the greatness of multicolored pens and comfortable jeans. Or saying "heck yeah!" to lemon shakeups and treats from the ice-cream truck. Or painting my toes purple. Or swinging on the swings. I mean, I can do all that stuff as long as it's before 9:00 p.m. Because, I am a forty-something after all. Let's not go crazy here.

Opportunity for Howling

How can you appreciate your version of grown up?

Write a love letter to yourself—and don't hold back! Just like
you would write to a new love in your life, write to yourself.
Compliment just what a completely spectacular human being
you've become, and be sure to use lots of examples of just why
you're so darn amazing. Hearts and other doodles to the side are
optional.

The Spark

Dear World

Dear World,
#%@#*!!!!! %&*#@$@*&*$%!!!!!!!!!!!!!
$#@@@$*&*$%#@!!!!!!!!!!!!!!!!!!!!!!!!!!!!!!!!!!!!!! !!!!!!! !
Love,
Erika

But seriously.

It seems that anytime I turn on the news, I start thinking about the overwhelming, well, "life-ness" of life. It's almost too much to bear sometimes, all this life. Because it's *all* always happening, isn't it?

For example, once I watched a dear young colleague lose her father in tragic circumstances, wrapped up in layers and layers of the complexities that come with families. I watched another colleague forced to "choose" between the family she was born into and the beautiful family she's created. I watched neighbors suddenly finding their long and independent life over, moving to a care facility after a single fall resulted in a broken hip that signified a break in life as they knew it. I watched, through the social blogosphere, a woman lose her five-year-old son after chronicling the story of his hard life, marked with serious health issues, and another mother write about her seventeen-year-old daughter who took her own life after being raped and then bullied for it. All this was punctuated at the same time by the bombing at the Boston Marathon.

But during that same time, I also bore witness to another colleague reveal a pregnancy that had been hard fought to achieve. I got a glimpse of a colleague's wife finding a new career direction that matched her incredible artistic talents with her love of parenting. I watched a video made by the students at one of the high schools we serve, designed to promote their urban production of *Les Miserables*, feeling the absolute pride and inspiration that comes from finding, and having the opportunity to showcase, your voice. I watched a new relationship blossom. And in the midst of the tragedy in Boston, I watched, along with thousands others, the heroes among us who ran *toward* the chaos in search of someone to help.

And of course, life is not just chronicled by the big moments of joy and pain, either. Regular old life goes on every day too. The kids need to be fed, reports need to be turned in, laundry needs doing, obligations must be met.

Ah, Dear World.

The dictionary defines the word "dear" as meaning "beloved or loved," "cherished," and "precious in one's regard." I hold this world precious, that's what it comes down to, and I am brought to my knees by the horrors and joys and just-so moments all contained within this dear, dear world.

In her book *Daring Greatly*, Brené Brown writes, "Much of the beauty of light owes its existence to the dark. The most powerful moments of our lives happen when we string together the small flickers of light created by courage, compassion, and connection and see them shine in the darkness of our struggles."

Opportunity for Howling

Can you string together the small flickers of light in your dear, dear world today?

When the darkness of the world feels overpowering, where do you find your light? How can you howl in the midst of all that is a part of this dear world?

The Spark

On Howling

We have one very precious and exquisite life at our hands, and if we wait for "it" to come to us, we will spend our days doing just that—waiting.

Do you ever have phases where life is juicy? Where there are plenty of opportunities to stop waiting and instead just show up—to say YES, to meet new people, join new communities, explore new opportunities—even if you're unclear on where those paths may lead? I don't know about you, but I find those phases in life to be exciting and fulfilling and also exhausting. Not to mention vulnerable—to put yourself out to the world's table and say "I'm here, I'm ready for the ride!" takes an enormous output of energy and courage. It can be tempting (for me at least) to crawl under the covers and just let life do its thing without your participation, hoping somehow it might throw you a bone as it saunters by.

But the thing I've discovered is that life *will* throw you a bone, but if you don't actively grab it, it will quickly disappear. Opportunities present themselves every day, but they also pass us by every day.

I am continually reminded that in this life there is no great reveal around the corner; there is no discovery on down the road; there is only what we make and remake. If we are seeking adventure, we must put one foot in front of the other. If we have a passion, we must share it. If we find our one unique contribution, we must offer it. We can easily choose to be spectators on the sidelines of our life rather than jumping into the game. But holy WOW, when we do join in. The knocks may be harder, but the rewards are bigger, too.

As Kid President (the phenomenal creation of Brad Montague and Robby Novack) says, "We were made to be awesome. Let's get out there! I don't know everything—I'm just a kid. But I do know this: It's everybody's duty to give the world a reason to dance."

So, let's start dancing.

Opportunity for Howling

How can you howl today?

First, howl. Actually howl. Give it your best shot—whether you do it in the privacy of your home or whether you step outside and wildly howl to the morning or night sky. Howl loudly, howl with abandon. (If you're anything like me, when you do this, you will feel absolutely absurd and embarrassed and fairly foolish. And then if you do it anyway, you will sheepishly look around to see if anyone noticed. And then you will feel a tickling, giddy feeling start to spread through your chest and will somehow feel somewhat *lighter*, as if the howl actually released some invisible weight.)

Next, write about ways you can "howl" in life—at work, in your relationships, in your choices, with your community.

Chapter Six: Celebrate

Overview

Why do we so often forget to celebrate a thing? And why is it that the person we often do the worst job celebrating is ourselves? To celebrate is to rejoice, and so in that way we have to wrap up this book by rejoicing in you.

Before we dive in, pick a page in your journal to paste images, drawings, pictures, and words to create a collage that represents CELEBRATE to you.

The Spark

Yay Me!

Just before my son turned two, he went through a phase of being quite self-congratulatory. I remember one morning when he woke up singing the "ABC" song, and it went something like this: "Ah-B-C-C-B-D-A-Eh-Eh-Eh... ... ... YAY DYLAN!!!!"

"Yay Dylan!" could often be heard around our house those days. If he threw something away in the trash or chased his sister or cleaned up a mess or figured out how to do anything on his own, you can bet he would celebrate that with a "YAY DYLAN!" or, at the very least, an "I DID IT!"

My husband and I would laugh about it, and thought that we could probably all take a cue from his actions. Why wait for someone else to praise you? Did you finish a report? Do the dishes? Build a shelf? Run the vacuum? Find a solution? Well, why not take a moment to throw up your hands with a hearty "YAY (insert your name here)!"

Now, while a robust and vocal congratulatory self shout-out might make others turn their heads and keep a safe distance, I do think there is something to this. How often do we wait to get our worth handed to us by someone else—a boss, a spouse, a friend? The need for external validation is so powerful that sometimes it feels like something isn't *good* until someone else says it's so. When I looked at that through the eyes of my almost-two-year-old, who proudly marched around the house declaring himself AWESOME at every turn, I think *he* was the one who had it right.

The other interesting thing about it is, because my son found it so fun to congratulate *himself* on every super cool thing he did, he also loved to congratulate all the rest of us. If he caught any of us doing something neat, the sounds of "YAY, MOMMY!" or "YAY, DADDY!" or "YAY, MARLOWE!" were also just as likely to ring through the house.

Genuine love for self, which is what I saw in Dylan and his delight in learning, discovering, and doing new things, is different from arrogance. Genuine self-love is not restrictive; rather, it's expansive.

So go on, get to loving yourself. Don't wait for others to tell you you're "good." I bet what you'll find is that you not only feel better about yourself, but that the world, and the people in it, start to look better too.

Opportunity for Celebration

Where can you say "YAY ME!" today?

Try this. Pick one day that will be your "YAY ME" day. Get a fresh pad of sticky notes and a pen to keep with you for the entire day. From the moment you wake up, each time you do something "YAY ME" worthy—whether it is not spilling your coffee or getting your report in on time or smiling at your grumpy partner—write it on a sticky note. For example, "YAY ME FOR REMEMBERING TO PACK MY CHILD'S LUNCH!" At the end of the day, post all of your sticky notes in your journal. Maybe even create an entire section that will be your ongoing YAY ME celebration, and refer to it whenever you need a reminder that you are more than enough, just as you are.

The Spark

On Grace and Gratitude

After a quick stop in Connecticut at the end of a business trip to New York, I headed back down to the city on the Metro North train. I was absentmindedly staring out of the window, when we passed an enormous billboard towering above some high-rise apartment buildings and automotive shops in the South Bronx. It had obviously been up for a while. Weathered and faded, it contained just one word: "Grattitude" (with an extra *t* to give that gratitude some attitude).

Grattitude.

Something about the starkness of it made me catch my breath. I wondered how many people living in that section of the South Bronx ever looked up to the sky and noticed that billboard. I wondered how many of the daily commuters hustling into the city from the outer reaches of New York and Connecticut ever looked up from their phones and laptops in time to see that billboard. I wondered how long it had been there, who put it there, and whether there had been more to the message long before time and the elements wore it down to its simplest form.

I happened to see that sign shortly after turning forty. Marking that occasion, I was already feeling an incredible amount of gratitude that I could count the ones I loved on both hands and that my entrance into that new decade was filled with an abundance of laughter, an outpouring of love, and even a shiny new pair of pink high top Chuck Taylors.

That birthday also triggered in me a great appreciation and respect for the fact that some birthdays—or any special occasion or holiday, for that matter—have the opposite effect. Some birthdays can painfully magnify feelings of loss, of want, of grief. Some birthdays remind us of failures or troubles. Some birthdays are spent alone. And on those birthdays and holidays that travel from bad to worse, where the collection of things that are *wrong* is so high that they form a wall impossible to see over, I wonder if it's possible for us to find the gratitude for any little thing within reach that might be *right.*

Hanging on the bulletin board next to my desk is a clipping from the November 2011 issue of *Real Simple* magazine which always helps to remind me where to look for what's *right.* An excerpt from G. K. Chesterton's *An Early Notebook,* it reads,

"You say grace before meals.
All right.
But I say grace before the play and the opera,
And grace before the concert and pantomime,
And grace before I open a book.
And grace before sketching, painting,
Swimming, fencing, boxing, walking, playing, dancing;
And grace before I dip the pen in the ink."

Our lives might be occasionally marked by big occasions, but they are so much more than that. They are a roller coaster of highs and lows, peaks and dips, starts and stops. What I feel in abundance today might disappear tomorrow. Some years it is easy for me to find the things I feel grateful for. But in the years where it isn't, I can remember to find grace in the small things—even an unexpected billboard with a powerful reminder.

Opportunity for Celebration

What can you say grace to today?

Contemplate the big and small things that you can have "grattitude" for today (gratitude with an attitude), especially things that feel hard or scarce. Can you find gratitude amid a disagreement? Can you find gratitude within a stressful situation? Can you find the gratitude that lies in the middle of disappointment?

The Spark

Somethings

I'll never forget the day my siblings and I said our final good-bye to our father. Just a few days after Christmas in 1998, the four of us traveled to a red covered bridge atop a creek in southern Indiana that was beloved by my father. Though I'd traveled across that creek countless times in a canoe, these circumstances were obviously quite different.

My dad had not wanted any formal service; he only wanted to be cremated and have the four of us, his children, sprinkle his ashes into this creek via one very specific covered bridge. So on a gray and blustery winter day, we found ourselves standing awkwardly on the bridge, holding a large box that contained our father's ashes.

This is how I remember it.

My brother was holding the box in one hand and a cigarette in the other. Alone on the bridge, the sole occupants of the area, we were all standing there shuffling about, trying to figure out how to ceremonialize what we were about to do. Suddenly, a car pulled up into the parking lot, startling us into action. As it happens, disposing of human ashes into public rivers is not altogether legal, so my brother quickly put the cigarette in his mouth, popped open the box, and chucked dad into the river.

Now. I don't know about you, but I would expect a large box full of ashes dumped into the wind to immediately scatter into a thousand different directions, whipped up into the sky and beyond. But that is not what I saw happen, at all.

Instead, what I saw was those ashes stay together in a large silvery gray cluster and land in the creek below. And you know what? Once they hit the water, those ashes *still* stayed together and floated down the creek until we couldn't see them anymore. In my mind's eye, I can clearly see them sparkling and dancing together among the rocks and ripples of the water. Whether you believe in the afterlife or a higher power or magic or witchcraft or nothing at all, I will swear to the end that I witnessed something. That something was be-au-ti-ful. Magical. Kind of indescribable.

And here's something else: That something that I experienced on that blustery winter day when I said good-bye to my dad? Well, that's my something alone. My siblings have their own stories from that day, each as unique and personal as mine.

We all have our "somethings," those memories that we hold specific and true. The message we get from a friend or stranger at exactly the time we need it. The thing we see out of the corner of our eye. The dream that brings something into focus. The ghost stories. The chance encounters.

I think it's important to find gratitude in the somethings that we experience. To celebrate the things we can't quite explain, the things that are ours alone to hold, the things that reveal, if for only a moment, a universe larger than we could possibly imagine.

As Hamlet said, "There are more things in heaven and earth, Horatio, than are dreamt of in your philosophy."

Opportunity for Celebration

Are you allowing yourself to be open to the somethings?

Have you had any "something" moments, moments that you can't quite explain or that seem to have only happened to you? Honor them here.

The Spark

On Celebrating

Many of us are great at celebrating birthdays and special occasions—retirements and babies and promotions and graduations. We offer cards and cakes and candles and sentiments of love and appreciation. We bring flowers and balloons. We sing. We laugh.

But how often do we offer a genuine celebration for the not-so-momentous occasions? The quiet moments that mark the passing of time? Celebrations don't always have to be splashy and include cake (although a random cake on a Tuesday is never a bad thing). I think celebration can look like the clinking toast of your morning coffee mugs and a hearty hello to the day ahead. Celebration can be a tradition of "Taco Tuesdays." Celebration can mean a trip to the ice-cream shop to celebrate the end of another week successfully... well, just *gotten through*. Celebration can be putting on lipstick for no reason at all. Celebration can be cuddling with your loved ones on the couch and watching TV together. Celebration can be unexpected flowers to brighten someone's day. Celebration can be remembering your coworker's favorite drink and bringing it to him. Celebration can be the words of love and gratitude coming out of your mouth. Celebration can be a hug. Celebration can come from saying YES to dessert before dinner or NO to the dreaded evening bath. Celebration can be making the choice to step outside and feel the warm sun rather than stay shuttered inside with your thoughts. There are opportunities for celebration everywhere, every day.

I understand that when life is on our side, when things are in order—whether it's our health, our family, our jobs, our relationships—in those moments it is an easier task to find ways to incorporate celebration into our day to day. But when things are hard, when we're struggling with loss, financial strains, anxiety, uncertainty—in *those* moments it can be tempting to write off celebration as something to be done in better times. But I think it's actually in those moments that opportunities for celebration are vital—even if it's just remembering to be grateful for the breath that you are taking in, right now. To me, celebration can be as simple (and hard) as saying YES and THANK YOU to this life, to this day, to this precise moment.

Opportunity for Celebration

Look around you. What can you celebrate today?

Go back to the celebration collage you made at the start of this chapter. What would you add or change, if anything? Let the collage evolve and grow into a larger reflection of celebration.

Now, that commencement speech I asked you to jot notes about... why not write it fully? What have your heart and intuition been telling you? What surprises have shown up in your journal? What discoveries have you made? So, imagine that you are given the stage to give a commencement speech—whether you're speaking to kindergartners or college graduates or humanity at large. What is on your heart? What does the world need to know about living a life filled with wings & whimsy?

Journal

Little begins create ~magic.

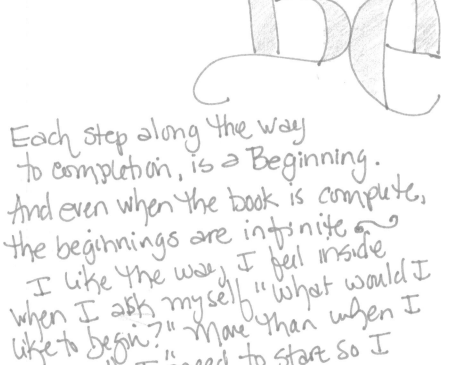

Each step along the way
to completion, is a Beginning.
And even when the book is complete,
the beginnings are infinite.
I like the way I feel inside
when I ask myself "what would I
like to begin?" More than when I
tell myself I "need to start so I
will finish."

Life is sometimes easy and sometimes hard and sometimes
boring and sometimes extraordinary. Live in all of it.

gin

Begin by:
- Contacting Salvia Yoon
- Cutting square paper and just write the words
- Keep the pages loose so they can come & go — shift and move
- Penal sketch the bigger environment the Tidbits live in.
- Write little vinyette of each Tidbits "activity" and the giving Tidbit's observation

Cup of golden sun:

- hand lettering
- the letter g
- magical happenings
- heart/soul connections
- getting into bed
- crisp air
- dusk
- the clouds in the sky to the east
- inspiration
- sketching nature
- watercolors
- Europe
- Riding my bike downhill
- the sound of water over rocks
- taking pictures
- making new friends
- the magical mystery of life
- discovering & evolving
- sharing
- chocolate & strawberry together
- stars
- sandpipers
- genuine smiles
- my Dad

- learning
- being alone
- being in love
- hand holding
- kissing
- cooking with music
- my studio
- green beans on the vine
- being thoughtful
- being strong & lean
  but maybe accepting change
- wood

crazy
over wheight
people

negative
talk

I do
eat what I want.
Say yes to "I deserve"
instead of yes to learn me
I don't like saying No
to me!

Focusing on scarcity is just too easy; I would rather focus on abundance.

If you don't risk the horrible pain of walking away empty-handed,
you will never know the exquisite joy of having your arms
overflowing with more than you ever wished for.

We paint a picture of what our lives should look like based on the pictures we see of other lives, but pictures capture moments, not lives.

In this life there is no great reveal around the corner; there is no discovery on down the road; there is only what we make and re-make. If we are seeking adventure we must put one foot in front of the other. If we have a passion we must share it. If we find our one unique contribution, we must offer it.

I will keep at it, every day. I will show up, arms wide open, gloriously trying.

My biggest wish for you, is that you wake up each morning with a content heart because you've surrounded yourself with people that you love, doing the things that you love, in a place that you love. May you keep joy as the north star of your compass as you navigate this easy, hard, boring, and extraordinary life. Because even if you are blessed enough to have a very long life, life goes by in a blink. Fill it up.

I think sometimes people equate the "truth" with the "facts." But the problem with that is that facts are just the quantifiable things that happen. Stories are what we do with those facts, and our lives are woven by our stories.

Life goes on. The best we can do is simply show up, try our best, try again, forgive ourselves, forgive others, enjoy the love moments, remember that the horror moments won't last forever, laugh as much as possible, and remind ourselves that perfection is an illusion.

Because THIS is life. Life is happy and grumpy; messy and clean; appreciative and bitter; tears and laughter. It is petty annoyances and earth-shattering moments. It is coffee and it is cathedrals. Sometimes life is long and sometimes life is much, much too short. Life is an ocean of everything— the things we take for granted and the things we remember to love fiercely. The things we notice and the things we lose sight of. It's amazing, this life. Every part of it. So rather than berating myself for not appreciating it more, for not doing it "better," instead I am just going to look around at the "everything" of it and just take a moment to say WOW.

Genuine self-love is not restrictive; rather, it's expansive.

Epilogue

On Wings & Whimsy

Today's society pushes for us to be extraordinary in all things.

We compete to be the heads of companies or countries, and we sometimes resort to ugly and deceitful tactics to get there.

We compete to win the championship and be known as the best, and that pressure can lead us to use drugs or other enhancements to get us there faster.

We push to get our kids into the best school and give them an edge, and in doing so we can unintentionally teach them that our love is attached to their performance.

We go to ridiculous lengths for fame and riches, and for our fifteen minutes we allow ourselves to compromise our integrity and our values.

We strive to keep up with the increasingly rapid pace of social media and connections—posting our status on Facebook; showcasing how we're going to decorate our house on Pinterest; sending a quippy, cleverly worded tweet on Twitter; snapping a dashing photo and instantly posting it with Instagram; proclaiming our exact location in the universe via Foursquare.

But what does it really mean to be extraordinary? To have the biggest salary, the most medals, the largest amount of "friends," the top hits on YouTube? Sometimes maybe those things happen to an extraordinary person, but those things do not *make* one extraordinary. To me, being extraordinary is more often than not about living our lives as *ordinarily* as possible—showing up for each authentic moment and giving it our best shot. Forgetting about what our "friends" think while making sure we are tending to our *friends*. Letting go of our dogged pursuit of the medal and remembering instead to just have fun in the race. Not obsessing over how we look to the world but rather focusing on what we're *contributing* to the world. To be extraordinary we must first remember to be extra-*ordinary*.

Go back and read through your past reflections and activities throughout your journal. How can you live your life as extra-ordinarily as possible, on flights of wings & whimsy?

So, that's it! We've come to the end. Thanks again for traveling along with me. And though we've come to the end, remember that endings are just the beginnings of something new—a commencement. So I'll leave you as we began:

Congratulations on this commencement. And may whatever is about to begin be simply breathtaking.

Credits

Andreas, Brian. *StoryPeople*

Brown, Brené. *Daring Greatly: How the Courage to Be Vulnerable Transforms the Way We Live, Love, Parent, and Lead.* New York, NY: Gotham Books, 2012. Print.

Brown, Brené. "The Power of Vulnerability." TED. Dec. 2010. Lecture.

Chesterton, G.K. *Orthodoxy.* New York: Dodd, Mead & Co., 1908. Print.

Chesterton, G.K. *The Collected Works of G.K. Chesterton: Volume X: Collected Poetry, Part I.* Ignatius Press, 1994. Print.

Gershwin, George and Ira. "Let's Call the Whole Thing Off." *Shall We Dance.* RKO, 1937.

Kid President. Dir. Brad Montague. Perf. Robby Novak. SoulPancake, 2015.

Over the Rhine. "The Song That Changed My Life". BYUtv. 2 Jul. 2012. Television.

Rodgers, Richard and Hammerstein, Oscar. "Do-Re-Mi." *The Sound of Music.* Sony Music, 1959.

Rowling, J.K. *Harry Potter and the Prisoner of Azkaban.* New York: Arthur A. Levine Books, 1999.

Shakespeare, William. *Hamlet.* Act 1, Scene 5: line 187-188).

About The Leadership Program:

The Leadership Program has been nationally recognized for our curricula and our engagement and motivation strategies. We teach children and adults to be self-aware, to express themselves, and to develop the skills needed to interact with one another and the outside world in a positive, pro-active way. Through this process we help shape environments that cultivate personal and social development. Our methodology fosters cultures of curiosity, open-mindedness, learning, and growth. We repeatedly witness that these types of cultures increase productivity, communication, resilience, interpersonal dynamics, capacity for healthy risk, and overall wellbeing. In all, Leadership prepares individuals, teams, and organizations to positively change their lives and communities, demonstrating that they can achieve and become everything they envision by delving into their potential, and stepping into their leadership.

About Erika:

Erika Petrelli is the Senior Vice President of Leadership Development (and self-declared Minister of Mischief) for The Leadership Program, a New York City-based organization. With a Masters degree in secondary education, Erika has been in the field of teaching and training for decades, and has been with Leadership since 1999. There she has the opportunity to nurture individual leadership spirit in both students and adults across the country. The legacy Erika strives daily to create is to be the runway upon which others take flight. One of the roles that truly ignites her is writing her weekly blog, which is how this book was born. She lives in Indiana with her family, and believes that the only things worth doing in life are the things that fill your soul and make you laugh, and that play and work must always go together.

Meet The Wings & Whimsy Team!

Erika Petrelli, Minister of Mischief

Ali Mercier, Dream Doer

Phil Caminiti, Doodle & Design Dealer

Lucille Rivin, Detail Diva

Thom Holme, Media Master

Tatiana Dominguez, Fan Flamer

To read hundreds more of Erika's stories like the ones
contained in this book, visit

www.tlpnyc.com/wings-and-whimsy

To learn more about the work of The Leadership
Program, visit

www.tlpnyc.com

Made in the USA
San Bernardino, CA
17 March 2017